THE PRACTICAL BOOK OF
BUILT-IN FURNITURE

Books By

HENRY LIONEL WILLIAMS

OLD AMERICAN HOUSES AND HOW TO RESTORE THEM
(*with* OTTALIE K. WILLIAMS)

MODERNIZING OLD HOUSES (*with* OTTALIE K. WILLIAMS)

THE PREFABRICATED HOUSE

HOW TO FURNISH OLD AMERICAN HOMES (*with* OTTALIE K. WILLIAMS)

EVERYWOMAN'S GUIDE TO HOUSEHOLD REPAIRS
(*with* OTTALIE K. WILLIAMS)

HOW TO MAKE YOUR OWN FURNITURE

THE CALENDAR GUIDE TO HOME REPAIRS

NEW ROOMS FOR OLD (*with* OTTALIE K. WILLIAMS)

An attic apartment made with sheetrock and built-in pieces.

An attic apartment made with sheetrock and built-in pieces.

THE PRACTICAL BOOK OF

BUILT-IN FURNITURE

By

Henry Lionel Williams

GRAMERCY PUBLISHING COMPANY • NEW YORK

This edition published by Gramercy Publishing Co.,
by arrangement with the author

O   P   Q   R   S

PRINTED IN THE

UNITED STATES OF AMERICA

CONTENTS

CHAPTER   PAGE

1. EVERY HOME NEEDS BUILT-INS 11
   Room Planning 12
   The Value of Planning Built-Ins 13
   Reorganizing Existing Storage 14

2. CONSTRUCTION METHODS 15
   Elementary Details — processes, tools 15
   Method of Joining 15
   Plywood Edges — how to hide 19
   Joining Board Edges 19
   Joint Fastenings — use of nails, gluing 20
   Legs and Brackets 21
   Facing of Board Edges 21
   Fastening Built-ins to Walls, Ceilings, and Floors . . 23
   Building to Bad Walls 25
   Attic Problems 26

3. CONSTRUCTION DETAILS FOR PARTS OF BUILT-IN
   UNITS 28
   Shelves 28
   Table and Counter Tops 30
   Drawers 32
   Frames for Paneled or Glazed Doors 33
   Matching Doors to Frames 35
   Sliding Doors 37

4. CONSTRUCTION DETAILS FOR TYPICAL BUILT-IN
   UNITS 40
   Bathroom Medicine Chest and Dresser 40
   Bed Base 42
   Workshop Tool or First-Aid Cabinet 43
   Floor Storage Box 43
   Garage or Basement Cupboard 45
   Sink and Counter for Potting Shed 46

Window Dressing-Table and Shelf Unit 47
Box-Type Seat 50
Dressing Unit 51
Wall Niche 52
Adding on to Built-in Units 53
Basic Kitchen Cabinet 56

5. ROOM-BY-ROOM BUILT-INS TO MAKE 59

Series 1. KITCHEN 59
Combination Kitchen Cabinet 59
Sink Cabinet and Counter 62
Stove Cabinet 64
Housekeeper's Desk 64
Back-of-Door Racks 67
Divided Shelves 67
Bread Board or Pull-Out Shelf 68
Ironing-Board Storage 71

Series 2. DINING ROOM 71
Partition Cabinetwork 71
Wall Box 71
Apartment-Type Dining Unit 73
China Cabinet 76
Corner Cupboard 76
Dining Room–Living Room Archway Fillers . . . 81
Complete Closure by Cabinet 82
Door with Cabinet Each Side 83
Reducing Opening with Decorative Panels . . . 85
Archways into Walls 85

Series 3. LIVING ROOM 87
Wall or Partitioning Multi-Purpose Unit 87
Radio, Phonograph, Record-Storage and Drawer Unit . 88
Simple Bookcase 90
Window-Wall Storage and Display Combination . . 90
TV Set and Projector-Screen Unit with Storage Space . 92
Free-Standing Shelf and Cabinet Built-in 92
Lightweight Room Divider Unit 96

Series 4. BEDROOMS 97
Bunk Beds 97
Bunk Bed–Desk Combination 97
Convertible Sofa-Bunk 101
Twin Bed Head Storage Unit 101

Series 5. BATHROOMS 102
General Utility Combination Built-in 102
Tub Separator with Canopy 105
Dresser Located at Window 105
Nest of Swinging Drawers 106
Legless Dresser 106
Laundry Bin and Wash-Basin Counter 107

Series 6. ATTIC 109
Dead Storage 109
Bedroom with Cabineting and Box-Type Beds . . . 109
Bedroom with Cabinets and Semi-Slideaway Beds . . 112

6. LUMBER AND MANUFACTURED SHEET STOCK . . 113
Lumber 113
Plywood and Other Laminated Sheets 114
Hardboards 116
Moldings 116

7. FINISHING AND COLORING 118
Application of Liquid Finishes 118
Plastic Veneers 120

INDEX 123

Series 4. BEDROOMS 97
    Bunk Beds 97
    Bunk Bed–Desk Combination 97
    Convertible Sofa-Bunk 101
    Twin Bed Head Storage Unit 101

Series 5. BATHROOMS 102
    General Utility Combination Built-in 102
    Tub Separator with Canopy 105
    Dresser Located at Window 105
    Nest of Swinging Drawers 106
    Legless Dresser 106
    Laundry Bin and Wash-Basin Counter 107

Series 6. ATTIC 109
    Dead Storage 109
    Bedroom with Cabineting and Box-Type Beds . . . 109
    Bedroom with Cabinets and Semi-Slideaway Beds . . 112

6. LUMBER AND MANUFACTURED SHEET STOCK . . 113
    Lumber 113
    Plywood and Other Laminated Sheets 114
    Hardboards 116
    Moldings 116

7. FINISHING AND COLORING 118
    Application of Liquid Finishes 118
    Plastic Veneers 120

INDEX 123

THE PRACTICAL BOOK OF
BUILT-IN FURNITURE

CHAPTER 1

Every Home Needs Built-Ins

EVERY home needs built-in units of various kinds. Even when there isn't a lack of storage space — of which few homes ever have enough — built-ins can be the answer to the problem of cutting the cost of furnishing. And that's not all. Besides taking the place of movable furniture, and saving money in the process, they can utilize otherwise unused space, or substitute order for wasteful untidiness. Furthermore, with built-in units you can remodel almost any interior. You can convert one room into two. You can fill in openings, construct seats, beds, dressers, kitchen counters and so on, utilizing both wall and floor space for storage of all kinds. You can make usable rooms of bare attics and cellars and turn odd corners in the garage into storage or working space.

Often, simple structures can be used as backgrounds for the regular furniture and serve to hide undesirable architectural features. As everyone knows, a house with too much furniture is congested and cluttered, unattractive and unpleasant to live in. By substituting built-in pieces you can get equivalent service and at the same time release floor space.

The success of any built-in unit is determined not only by its utility but also by the way it blends in with the rest of the room. No well-designed built-in piece should look like an afterthought, or something stuck on in a hurry. In other words, the less a built-in piece looks built-in, the more it enhances the beauty of the room you put it in. The final test is whether or not it appears as though it had always belonged. Is it an essential part of the whole furnishing scheme?

In planning all such additions it is necessary to keep in mind the complete, furnished room. You have to remember that tall units and deep ones will make a room look smaller; that odd-shaped units and projections can give a room an untidy look and throw it out of balance. In many instances this calls for special treatment either to subdue or emphasize certain features.

Another advantage offered by built-in pieces is that space can be economized and clutter reduced by incorporating loose units into the pieces themselves, such as storage boxes in beds, chairs in kitchen counters, and so on.

The only possible drawbacks to permanently attached built-ins are that ordinarily you can't take them with you; they may not suit a new owner of the house, and they need planning for the type of furniture they are to go with and form a background for. Once attached, they cannot be changed around as loose furniture can. For this reason it is advantageous sometimes to make the built-ins detachable or even free-standing.

It usually is best to attach the built-in pieces firmly to the house structure, but you can use screws or bolts that can be removed readily without seriously damaging the walls, ceilings, or floors. You may want to change things later on. Or if you sell the place the new owner may not want them. And he certainly won't relish tearing the house apart to dislodge your handiwork.

On the other hand, building into a space, and attaching more or less permanently, generally simplifies construction and provides strength and solidity at lower cost. The whole thing therefore merits careful planning and consideration.

Room Planning

In deciding what built-ins you need it pays to survey the room in question and see what the basic cause of clutter actually is. Sometimes furniture rearrangement will help, but in any case there are some excellent guides to go by. It has been found, for instance, that traffic lanes through rooms should be 30 inches wide; 36 inches is the average space needed to open a drawer; there should be 54 inches seating space between a table and a wall; 6 to 12 inches between a chair and ottoman; 36 inches chair space between a desk and the wall; and 15 inches knee space at a coffee table.

With your furniture arranged to these minimums you can see what you have room for and what other provision you need to make to get the best out of that room.

Most of us need to be careful in separating things we need access to often from those we need only occasionally. In other words, it pays to make separate provision for active storage and dead storage. The fact that we may rarely do this is responsible (for example) for kitchens that are crammed with ceiling cupboards full of items and gadgets that are used no more than once a year. The result is an unpleasing appearance and far too little air space, actual or apparent. The remedy is to store such things elsewhere. This means planning — and often the exercise of ingenuity — so that the built-in pieces can be designed for some specific purposes and not just as catchalls.

The Value of Planning Built-ins

In designing your cupboard and closet built-ins remember that capacity is more important than overall size! With careful planning you can economize space and so save time and lumber and do a better job. Here are some standard unit sizes that may help you in laying out cabinet or cupboard space.

Bookcases

Average books need only 10 inches between shelves; some larger books will need 12 inches.

Kitchen Shelves

Ordinary dinner plates need shelves 12 inches deep (back to front). In some instances, slanting shelves in shallow cupboards will accommodate larger pieces. For very large pieces, including trays, use vertical racks either back-to-front or transverse. You will need about 16 square feet of shelf space to store china and glassware sufficient for 6 people.

Desks

Top height varies from 28 to 30 inches.

Clothes Closets

Clothes hangers plus clothes require 24 inches depth.

Clothes can be stored without hangers in a 16-inch-deep closet. Clothes hooks should be 12 inches apart.

Children's hangers should be 48 inches above floor. Adults' hangers should be 60 inches above floor. Coveralls need hangers 72 inches above the floor.

A shelf in clothes closet should be 4 inches above hooks or $2\frac{1}{2}$ inches above the hanger rail.

On an average, each person needs 48 inches of rail space.

Cleaning Closet

Minimum size, 16 inches deep, 36 inches wide.

Reorganizing Existing Storage

In many cases lack of space is brought about by the family outgrowing the house. This often calls for reallocating space, regrouping of present storage facilities and doing things to make some furniture pieces take up less space or look a lot less bulky. It is astounding what you can do for a room by making such simple changes as bleaching a piano bench to reduce its importance; by turning the piano end-on to the wall and decorating its back so that it acts as a partition and sets off a group of furniture pieces. Floor space is saved by substituting folding, sliding or concertina-type doors. These are but a few of the things you should think about in planning built-in furniture. The important thing is the plan.

In the succeeding chapters you will find a wide variety of suggestions for built-in pieces. Plans for any of these units can be modified or changed to suit your special requirements as to space occupied, capacity and detail design. The most important thing is to select a design that not only will serve your purpose but also will fit into your present furnishing scheme.

Most built-ins should serve as backgrounds rather than objects for display in themselves. Some, however, such as storage walls incorporating radio, TV, phonograph, or writing-desk units, may be prominently featured in a room. In such cases, they need to follow the general style of the room and its furnishings. This may mean, on occasion, the selection of a design of unit that serves your purposes, then modifying its style to conform. As you will see, the major difference between traditional styles of built-ins and modern styles is largely a matter of decoration, and you can often adapt decorative ideas for the built-ins from your existing furniture and room details. In doing this you have the help of modern materials and devices, many of which are described and illustrated in the pages that follow.

CHAPTER 2

Construction
Methods

Elementary Details

IF you know how to fasten two pieces of wood together you can make anything shown in this book. This fact becomes obvious when it is shown that it takes no more skill to make a seemingly complicated cabinet or case than it does to make a small or simple one. The larger pieces actually are often no more than several small units combined. A cupboard with three doors and six shelves, for example, is no more difficult to plan and put together than a cupboard with one door and two shelves. They both call for the same elementary knowledge of the simplest woodworking operations — measuring, sawing, planing, sanding, gluing and the driving of nails and screws. The principal difference between the beginner and the expert is the accuracy with which they cut to a line and fit the parts together.

In some of these pieces you will need to know how to use a chisel and saw a curve, but these operations, too, will prove simpler than they seem at first. With the begin-

ning carpenter and joiner in mind, many of the operations have been simplified, and plain joints have been substituted for the more intricate ones used by some professionals.

It seems customary for the amateur carpenter to start out with hand tools, graduating to power tools only when he has mastered the use of the hand-saw, chisel and plane. What these beginners do not realize is that even a small bench saw can enable them to make *straight* cuts, both across and with the grain, and form accurate joints. Women in particular, with their weaker wrists, will find in such a power tool a means of cutting and shaping even the larger pieces of wood with the expenditure of practically no muscular effort.

Method of Joining

One of the first things to decide in planning any built-in furniture — whether it is to be attached permanently or temporarily, or merely free-standing — is the way it is

15

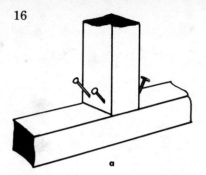

a

Toenailing vertical 2x4 to a horizontal one.

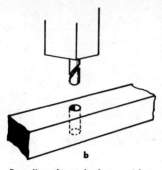

b

Doweling the end of one stick to the side of another.

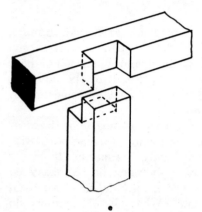

e

A halved joint held with glue and nails or screws.

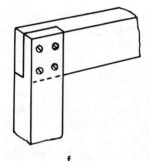

f

A halved corner joint often used in place of a mitered joint.

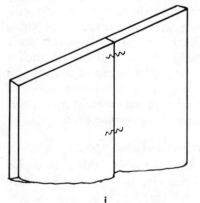

i

Corrugated nails are often used for joining the edges of two boards. The joint can also be glued.

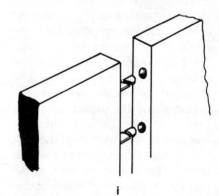

j

In better construction, board edges are glued and doweled.

Fig. 1

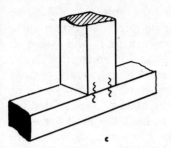

c

Joining two sticks with corrugated nails, two on each side.

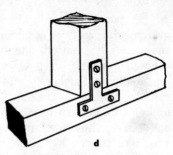

d

Fastening a right-angle joint with a metal T.

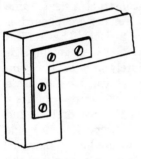

g

A square corner held with a metal angle.

h

Two corner joints made with corrugated nails. The right-hand one is mitered at 45 degrees.

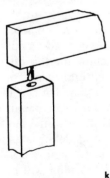

k

The dowel is often used in corner joints like this.

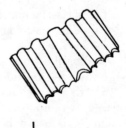

l

The corrugated nail. The sloping grooves pull the work together as it is driven in.

Fig. 1

to be put together. There are two general types of construction: the carefully jointed, glued and screwed assembly used by joiners and cabinet makers, and the rougher framing, boarding, and nailing of the carpenter. For the amateur — those men and women who like to do their own woodworking — a combination of both of these methods is usually simplest and best.

The built-in piece that is securely attached to the house structure is not subjected to the same stresses as a free-standing piece. It doesn't get pulled about or stood on end. When it is in position it stays there. This is one reason why many joints do not need to be as strong or rigid as those of a movable piece of furniture. It is only when you get to dealing with partition-type built-ins, or those that are only partially attached, that the extra strength and stiffness is needed. The point, then, is that building in simplifies construction, and fastening things to walls or other parts of a house calls for very little skill, once you understand the basic idea.

Ordinarily, the same outside appearance — and almost the same strength and rigidity — can be secured without the use of fancy joints, and reasonably careful planning of the construction can produce a satisfactory exterior that betrays no amateur workmanship. For example, instead of a mortise-and-tenon joint you can often use a dowel (or even a pair of dowels) and a little glue. For certain angle joints you can use L- and T-shaped screw plates or corrugated nails. Better results usually are secured with nailed or screwed joints in which the wood parts are fitted together without the need for extra devices. A number of joints are illustrated in Fig. 1.

The ability to put together a simple right-angle joint makes it possible to construct a neat frame to form the front of a cupboard or the frame of a door. The hardest part of such a job is getting the joints absolutely square. This simply means that you have to use a steel square, measure accurately to 1/16th of an inch or less, and saw along the proper (waste) side of the lines to produce a tight fit. But before you cut anything at all, make sure the space you are building into is also square. So often, especially in older houses, the walls will lean slightly or be out of square with ceiling or floor. In such cases you will need to cut your framing to allow for the difference in angle or dimension, or cover the gap with your trim. All of this calls more for care than it does for skill. Just take your time.

The next important detail is assembling the parts to assure firm joints. How rigid any joint will be depends largely on the amount of leverage it is likely to be subjected to. Sometimes you can get away with nailing through the side of one board into the edge of another.

Normally, however, you will need to make a stiffer joint by bracing the corner in some way. Fig. 2 shows one simple means of stiffening a hidden (inside) corner joint. The corner is filled with a wood block that is screwed to both boards. If the boards are thin you will need to screw through them into the block, and probably use glue as well.

Plywood Edge Treatment

Since plywood offers so many advantages in making built-ins, you need to know how to treat the rather undecorative edges. With thick plywood you can make a right-angle joint as in Fig. 3a, hiding the end inside grain of one sheet with the thin outer layer of the other one. Quite a different, but equally effective, method is to cover the grain with a hard coating of Swedish putty — a mixture of spackle and varnish that you can make yourself. A more professional job is done by banding (i.e., covering) the edges with wood strips as you see in the three examples in Fig. 3b. For this work you need clean, straight cuts, preferably made with a circular saw. Alternatively, you can often use a strip of thin stock molding, such as screen molding, glued or fastened with brads. Several moldings are available 3/16 inch to ⅜ inch thick, including glass-bead, quarter-round, parting stop, and a variety of beading. Some of these are available in fancy woods as well

as pine. You can get them at any good lumber supply or hardware store.

Joining Board Edges

When you have to join two or more narrow boards to make a wide

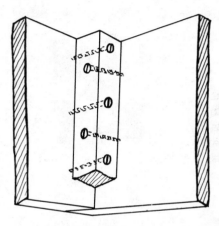

Fig. 2
Strong corners can be made with a square, glued strip screwed to both front and side pieces.

one — as in constructing a table top — you have several alternatives. You can glue square-edged or tongue-and-grooved (t & g) boards together; you can dowel the square-edged stuff together (as in Fig. 1j); or hold the boards in line with two or more battens (narrow strips of wood screwed or nailed across the joint). Boards that are glued or doweled can also be stiffened by applying cleats across their ends, the cleats being doweled or screwed into the end grain.

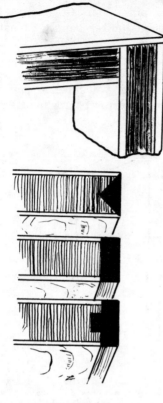

Fig. 3
Methods of hiding plywood end grain.

Joint Fastenings

There is a right way and a wrong way of joining any two pieces of wood. The method you use may make a great difference in the strength and rigidity of the built-in unit. Even the plain nailed joints call for the right kind of nails, properly inserted.

In making heavy frames — of 2x3s or 2x4s — it is best to use headed (common) nails because they hold better than headless (fin-

ishing) nails, and appearance at this stage of construction is not important. A nail holds because of the friction between it and the material in which it is embedded. Wood fibers grip the nail, and how well they grip depends largely on the density of the wood and the grain direction.

If you nail into end grain — i.e., into the end of a piece of wood — the joint will not be strong because the grain tends to separate instead of squeezing the nail. That is because the nail shank goes down between the wood fibers instead of cutting through them. So when you nail to the end of a piece of wood you need extra-long nails and the help of glue. Also, it pays to insert the nail at a slight angle. If the wood is tough, you can use fatter nails without splitting it. Whenever possible, nail through the face grain of the wood.

The value of a nail head is that it pulls the two pieces of wood together solidly, provided that enough of the nail shank is in the second piece of wood.

Finishing nails, which have hardly any head, are tidier to use because you can drive the head below the surface of the wood, where it is not seen. Then the hole is packed with some filler such as plastic wood or wood putty. Any nail you use should ordinarily be at least twice as long as the thickness of the first piece of wood it is driven through, and if it can be half as long again, so much the better.

Always try to nail through the thinner piece of wood into the thicker one.

If you have to fasten a thick piece of wood to a thin one so that you cannot use a long nail, it may be better to use a screw. Furthermore, if the joint is to be permanent, a little glue may hold better than either nail or screw. In fact, some of the strongest joints are made with glue alone. If you use a good waterproof glue such as Weldwood or Cascamite, the joint will probably be stronger than the wood around it, and the wood will break before the joint does.

In cases where you have to fasten into end grain, or the piece you are fastening needs to be held rigidly at one point, it may be best to use a screw and perhaps glue also.

Legs and Brackets

Going on now to basic structural details, it is useful to know that in many instances legs need not be made of solid wood. Quite strong supports are often made by joining two strips at right angles, as you see in Fig. 4. Another type of support you will commonly use is the shelf or wall bracket. It is a simple matter to cut a pair of brackets out of a square of wood as in Fig. 5. In cases where you cannot fasten such individual brackets firmly to a wall you may have to mount them on a backboard, as in Fig. 6. The board is then screwed to the wall studs or to plugs in a masonry wall. See Fig. 7.

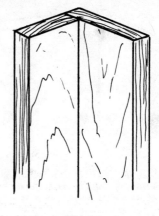

Fig. 4

In constructing cabinets, a pair of narrow strips can often replace a heavy 2x3 or 2x4 corner post.

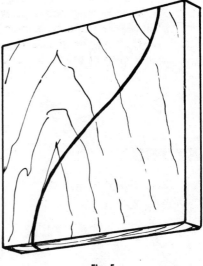

Fig. 5

Two shelf brackets cut from one square of wood.

Facing of Board Edges

In designing and making built-ins, two marks of the amateur are the lack of proportion and the absence of properly applied decora-

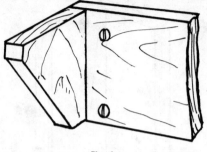

Fig. 6
Sometimes shelf brackets have to be attached
to a backboard, which in turn is nailed to wall
studs or screwed to plugs in a masonry wall.

tion. In making a bookcase, for
example, whether it is to be traditional or modern or just plain
utilitarian, the edges of the members need to be thick enough to
give an impression of strength and
solidity. If the wood is too thin,
the whole structure will look

skimpy and weak and quite unpro-
fessional. The side members should
be at least as heavy as the shelves,
and will look better if they are
heavier. Therefore, if you use thin
wood in the basic structure, plan
on hiding the edges by covering
them with a wider facing.

This facing, or trim, is applied in
the form of vertical and horizontal
pieces with the surface grain facing
outward. These can be 1½ inches
to 3 or even 4 inches wide accord-
ing to the proportions of the piece
and the effect desired. They are
nailed (with finishing nails), and
sometimes glued as well, to the
edges of the side members and partitions and perhaps to the top and
bottom also. Ordinarily, the horizontal pieces extend over the tops

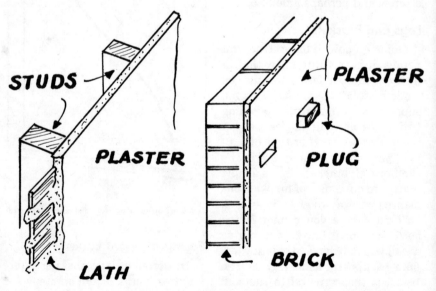

Fig. 7
Plaster wall construction (left). Brick wall with attachment plugs (right). Plugs are hammered
into holes cut in wall.

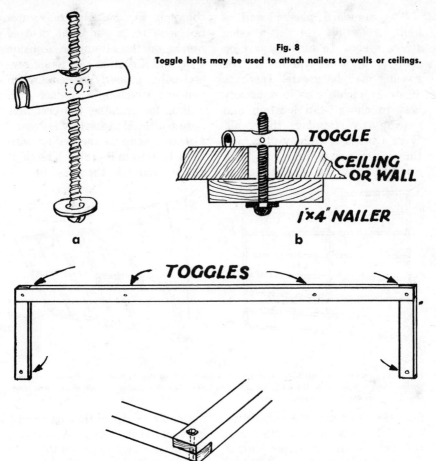

Fig. 8
Toggle bolts may be used to attach nailers to walls or ceilings.

TOGGLE

CEILING
OR WALL

1"x4" NAILER

a

b

TOGGLES

TOGGLE

c

and under the bottoms of the vertical ones, but in some instances it is better to miter the corners. Where the frame extends to the ceiling, it is customary to use quite a wide horizontal board, top and bottom. And in many cases the angle between the top rail and the ceiling is best covered with a piece of cornice or "sprung" molding.

Fastening Built-ins to Walls, Ceilings, and Floors

An important feature of most built-in pieces is the method used to attach them to walls, floor or ceiling. If this is done properly, there will be little damage to any surface, and the fixture will be removable without much trouble or necessary restoration.

The standard plaster wall is built on vertical 2x4-inch wooden studs, spaced 16 inches apart on centers. In some old houses the spacing may be greater (perhaps 19 or 24 inches), so it is usually best to check stud location and spacing by tapping the wall. With a brick or stone wall behind the plaster, you will have no thick wood to screw into and it may be

shown in Fig. 8a. Naturally, it is not wise to put a great deal of weight on the lathing in any one spot, and it is often best to use several bolts, properly spaced. When you are attaching a cabinet to a ceiling, for example, the best procedure often is to start by fastening a nailing strip to the ceiling with these bolts (see Fig. 8b). The cabinet structure is then fastened to

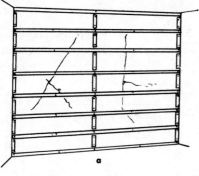 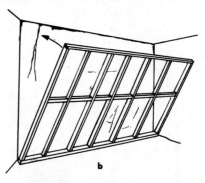

Fig. 9

Two ways to prepare a wall for boarding over or for attaching the back of a built-in unit. In (a), furring strips are nailed to the wall; (b) shows complete 2x3 stud frame assembled on floor, then raised and fastened in position.

necessary to provide a substitute. Normally, this means cutting into the wall — into a mortar joint if you can find it; if not, into the brick or stone. Drive a wooden plug into this hole and screw into that (see Fig. 7).

Where you have a plaster wall or ceiling it sometimes happens that you have to anchor to the plaster and lathing instead of to a joist or stud. In this case, you may be able to screw into the laths, but usually it is better to drill a hole through the plaster and lath and insert a toggle bolt of the kind

the nailing strip so that its weight is evenly distributed. Always, of course, it is best to fasten this supporting strip to a ceiling joist if possible.

Ceiling cabinets are also fastened to the wall, wherever possible, through a nailing strip. See Fig. 8c. This strip usually can be nailed directly to two or more studs. If the strip is located down from the ceiling at a distance equal to the thickness of the cabinet top, the top can rest directly on it. If the cabinet has no top, it may pay to install a supporting strip — perhaps a length of 1x3 — at the rear top of the cabinet. You can usually nail through this directly into the wall plate or girt which rests on top of the studs at ceiling level. In most instances you can also use a narrow supporting strip underneath the cabinet where it will not be obvious.

Building to Bad Walls

Quite often, in erecting built-in units, it is necessary to work over walls that are cracked, bulging or otherwise damaged. Such walls, as a matter of fact, offer a direct invitation to cover them with cupboards, closets, shelves or plain boarding. However, difficulties may arise from old, crumbling plaster as work is being attached to the studs. In such cases it may pay to cover the wall, partly or wholly, with a wooden framework to which the new surface or structure may be fastened. The two standard ways of doing this are: (a) to apply furring strips to the walls and (b) to cover the wall with a new framework (studding), with or without a new wall surface attached to it. Fig. 9 shows both of these methods. The furring (Fig. 9a) is suitable only for light loads, such as wallboards that are to serve as backing for shelves or simply as wall finish. Any other load would have to be anchored solidly to the wall studs directly. When you have big loads to support, and where you need a particularly straight and solid surface,

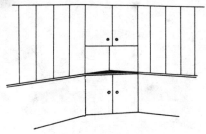

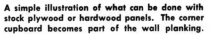

Fig. 10

A simple illustration of what can be done with stock plywood or hardwood panels. The corner cupboard becomes part of the wall planking.

the new stud framing is best.

Such a framing has to be made on the floor, then pushed erect into position as Fig. 9b indicates. However, if the ceiling bulges, this will not be possible. You may then have to cut down the height of the frame (perhaps by the thickness of a 2x4), then pack the space over it with an extra 2x4 after the frame is in position. This frame can be arranged to nail through to the original studs, but on a crooked wall the nailing could be confined to the floor and perhaps the original wall plate, using spacers where necessary. When the whole structure is square and solid, other spacers may be inserted between studs and wall, and the new studs toenailed to the old ones through them. In the end, you will have plenty of nailing surface whether the studding is covered with wallboard or not.

Fig. 10 shows a wall to which wood "panels" have been attached as part of a decorating scheme that incorporates a corner cupboard — all over furring. Where you have

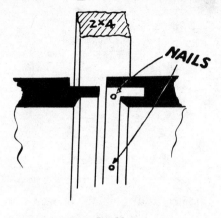

Fig. 11

Wall panels are easy to apply. Here is a simple method. Other types of board you can buy use metal clips.

install a new wall (in place of a room-divider built-in unit), this wallboarding can be fastened directly to the studs. No particular skill is needed for this. In Fig. 11 you see a typical wall-panel joint and the method of fastening it to the stud. You can get from your lumberman large sheets of this type of board, either painted or grained, 4 feet x 8 feet or over. Into both types of "paneling" you can introduce built-in units, small or large, and get a unified room of which the built-ins are an integral part. They don't look "stuck on."

hopelessly bad plaster walls that can be cured only by stripping off the plaster, or where you wish to

Attic Problems

Another wall problem sometimes arises in connection with attics.

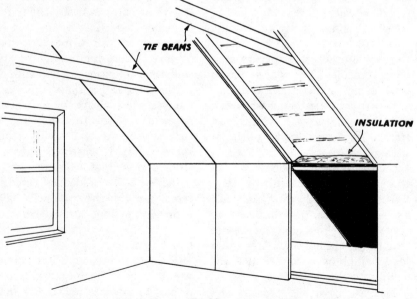

Fig. 12

If attic tie beams are too low, leave them exposed and enclose rafters up to the peak. A 4-foot wall provides storage space into which cupboards or drawers can be built.

Here you may have low tie-beams that make it unwise to attach the ceiling to their undersides. The alternative is to leave them open and board in the rafters as in Fig. 12. Any roof insulation must then be applied between the rafters and behind the boarding. In this type of roof nothing is gained by closing in the rafters all the way down to the wall plate. A much better appearance is obtained by walling off the rafter feet simply by erecting a wall about 4 feet high under the rafter slope, as in the sketch. This is done by erecting a frame of 2x4 lumber on which to nail wallboard. The space behind this wall need not be wasted. The 4-foot wall can be opened anywhere, with a 2x4 frame around the hole, and shelves, drawers or a cupboard built in. A simple access door lets you use the space for storage.

CHAPTER 3

Construction Details for
Parts of Built-In Units

Shelves

ONE of the commoner operations involved in making built-in furniture is the mounting of shelves. The sketches in Fig. 13 show several methods. The simplest way to get a level shelf that is strongly supported is to nail or screw (and perhaps glue) square strips of wood to the sides of the case (Fig. 13a). The shelf can then be laid on loosely or held with finishing nails. The drawback to this method is that the ends of the supports may be visible and detract from the appearance. Quarter-round strips (Fig. 13b) show less and make a neater job, as also does a piece of cove molding (Fig. 13c).

In any case, a more professional result is obtained by covering the front edge of each side with a vertical strip (Fig. 13d). Where this wide edge is not desirable (as in some modern designs) the shelf can be fitted into channels cut into the sides of the case (Fig. 13e). These channels (called dadoes), however, are not easy to cut across a wide

board without a bench saw. A practical alternative may be to hold the shelf with screws through the sides, the screws being countersunk into the wood and their heads covered with plastic wood. The drawback to this is that screwing or nailing into end grain is not always satisfactory. You may split the shelf board and you may not get a strong joint. A shelf attached in this manner contributes very little to the strength or rigidity of the structure.

A better way to support a shelf is to fasten a pair of vertical strips (say ¾ inch x 1 inch) to each side, at the edge (Fig. 13f). These strips would extend from one shelf to another, with gaps between their ends for the shelf board. Or you could use solid boards in place of the strips; these would give the effect of a dado (Fig. 13g).

If you need adjustable shelves it is easy to drill a series of holes in the sides to receive short pieces of dowel stick on which the shelf can

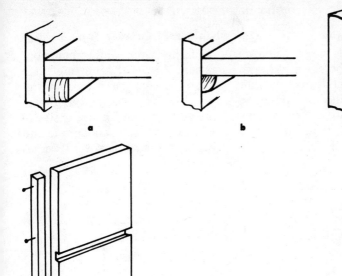

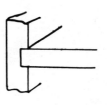

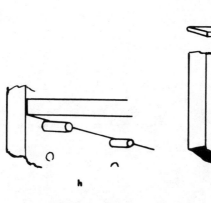

Fig. 13
Several ways of mounting shelves in a cabinet.

rest as shown in Fig. 13h. Also there are available simple screw-on shelf-supporting brackets, as shown in Fig. 13i, or metal brackets that fit into holes drilled in the sides. However, these two devices make a less secure shelf than the other methods described.

Table and Counter Tops

Another simple and common operation is that of attaching table or counter tops. Here, too, you can choose from a variety of methods. The vertical board under the edge of a top is called an apron, and usually it is fairly narrow. It serves

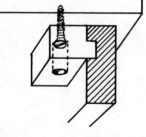

a

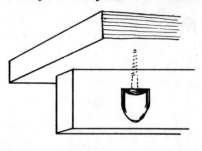

b

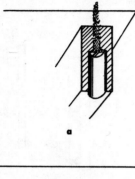

c

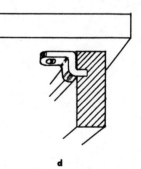

d

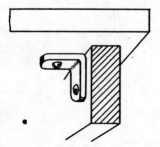

e

Fig. 14
Several methods of attaching a table top to its apron.

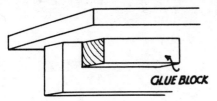

Fig. 15

Glue block reinforces joint between table top and apron.

apron that engages with either a wood or metal clip screwed to the top board (Fig. 14c and d); and by using metal angles (Fig. 14e).

In many such joints it pays to use what are known as glueblocks, as shown in Fig. 15. These are simple blocks of wood, preferably of a hardwood such as sycamore or maple, made to fit into the angle between the two surfaces to be joined. The two adjoining faces of the block are well glued. The block is then laid in position and rubbed back and forth an inch or so in the angle. This works the glue into both surfaces. The block is then left in place for the glue to set. If the piece is upright or must be moved, you can use a finishing nail to hold the block, or even clamp it, while the glue is drying. This should be avoided where possible since it may pull the block slightly away from one surface.

to stiffen the top, besides adding to the appearance, and therefore should be firmly attached to it throughout its length. The simplest way of joining the apron and top is to nail through the top down into the edge of the apron. But this is not usually recommended. In Fig. 14 you can see five ways of attaching an apron — by countersinking screws into the bottom edge of the apron (Fig. 14a); by recessing the screws in the inside face of the apron (Fig. 14b); by cutting a groove in the

Fig. 16

Assembling a drawer with (a) dovetail joints and (b) by rabbeting the front board to receive the sides.

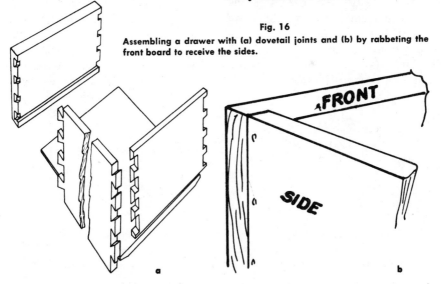

a

b

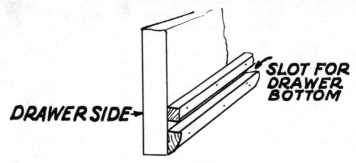

Fig. 17
You can use nailed-on strips to form slot for drawer bottom.

Drawers

The important item of drawer construction is one that calls for special attention.

The professional way to make a drawer is to use dovetail joints (Fig. 16a) front and back, grooving the sides to take the bottom. This is the best and strongest form of construction. However, a satisfactory drawer can be made without a dovetail — or even a groove. One alternative is to rabbet the front board to receive the sides, which are then glued and nailed in (Fig. 16b). Instead of cutting grooves in the sides and front to

receive the bottom, nail on strips of wood as you see in Fig. 17 and merely slide the bottom into them. The back likewise can be nailed between the sides, on top of the bottom board.

There is still another trick you can use. When the front of the piece you are making does not need to have an apron or drawer frame you can suspend the drawer by its sides as in Fig. 18a. Ordinarily you will make a pair of bottom slides for the drawer to run on and a pair of guides to keep it straight (Fig. 18b). With the side suspension system, the pair of slides, well

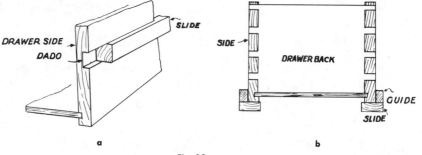

Fig. 18
You can suspend the drawer from its sides (a), or use bottom slides with guides (b).

waxed, will run in dadoes cut in the drawer sides. However, where the drawer sides are too thin to be dadoed, you can substitute for each groove either one wood strip or a pair of wood strips that form guides. The only problem here is that the guides come out with the drawer and you have to provide clearance for them on either side of the drawer opening. But this means only a wider opening, and a *wider drawer front* to cover the ends of the guides. In place of guides or slides you can use special rollers attached to the drawer base and back. You can buy these in sets ready to screw in place. Then all you need is a flat bottom for the drawer to roll over.

eled or glazed doors. Normally this calls for joining rabbeted strips of wood at right angles, with the rabbet forming a right-angled recess in the inside face of the frame, either front or back, to hold the panel. The location of the rabbet in relation to the front of the door, and its depth, are governed by the type of panel to be used.

If you have a miter-box it is easy to cut the frame corners at 45 degrees and so make a 90-degree (or "square") joint (Figs. 19a and b). It is also possible to make square joints as shown in Figs. 19c and d, or a combination of square and miter as in Fig. 19e. If you don't have a rabbet plane or power saw you can build up a rabbet by nail-

Frames for Paneled or Glazed Doors

Another common operation in making built-in furniture is the construction of the frames of pan-

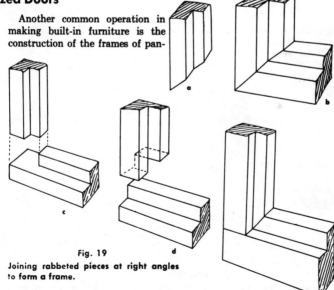

Fig. 19

Joining rabbeted pieces at right angles to form a frame.

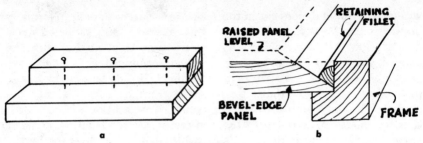

a

b

Fig. 20

Forming a rabbet with nailed-on strips (a); method of setting and securing raised panel in a rabbeted frame (b).

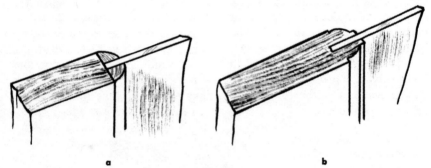

a

b

Fig. 21

A sunk panel may be held with quarter-round molding (a), or in a molded frame you can buy (b).

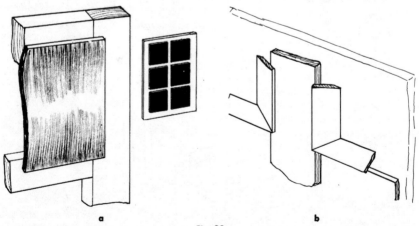

a

b

Fig. 22

(a) Procedure for making a raised-panel door; (b) frame strips and panels mounted on a wood surface.

ing and gluing a strip of wood to each frame member (Fig. 20a). But don't forget the location of the nails when you come to saw the strips to size! Usually it is far better to make the frame first, then insert the strips to form rabbets. This also has the advantage of enabling you to use quarter-round or more fancy molding at the front.

Wood, glass or decorative metal panels can consist of a single sheet of material set in a rabbeted frame either from the front or the back. The panel needs to be thin enough at the edges to leave a space within the thickness of the frame for retaining strips. If it is set in flush at the back it will need to be glued in place or have retaining strips applied to the back surface.

Raised panels are made by setting a thicker sheet of wood into a rabbeted frame so that its front surface is either flush with or projects beyond the face of the frame (Fig. 20b). If the face of the panel is flush with the face of the frame it will need to have beveled edges to give the raised appearance. In both cases the panel is usually set in from the front and retained by strips of molding. There is, however, no reason why it can't be set in from the back, and retained in the same manner. For a more modern effect, simulated raised panels are made by tacking thinner boards (either square-edged or beveled) to the face of a flush panel.

You can achieve still another paneled effect by fastening a thin sheet to the inside of a frame by means of quarter-round molding on both sides, all around the edges (Fig. 21a). You can also buy frame stock with the molding already formed on it (Fig. 21b).

You can apply the panels to the face of the frame (Fig. 22a). If you're making a fairly large door the frame can be divided into sections, and separate square sheets can be applied to form a series of panels. Finally, you can have an interesting deep-paneled effect (Fig. 22b) by mounting frame strips and panel moldings on another surface.

Matching Doors to Frames

Some door frames are rabbeted to receive the door when you close it. Therefore the wood of the frame must be thicker than the door. Rabbeted door frames are made in the same manner as the rabbeted frames just described. The door, when closed, fits flush with the outer face of the frame.

But most frames are not rabbeted, and the doors fit snugly inside them. In such cases there must be some method of preventing the door from going too far inside the frame when closed. The front edge of a shelf may serve, or a block inside the bottom lip, or any standard metal catch.

In many cabinets you can use doors that close against the front of the frame. All four edges of these doors are rabbeted, the rabbets concealing the clearance

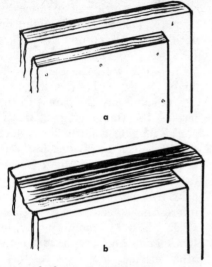

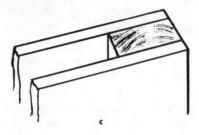

Fig. 23

Cabinet door made from two pieces of plywood joined to form a rabbet (a); a thick plywood door faced with fancy woods (b); a thick but light door consisting of two thin plywood sheets separated by strips between them.

around the opening between door and frame. To make doors of this type you can use either of the methods shown in Figs. 23a or b.

Fig. 23a shows a door made up of two sheets of thin plywood glued and nailed together. The smaller sheet is cut to fit inside the door frame; the larger one goes in front of it and forms a lip on all four sides that covers the joint when the door is closed. In Fig. 23b a thick piece of plywood is used, and all four edges are rabbeted. A special hinge is made for use with these lipped doors.

In Fig. 23c a thick but light door is made from two thin sheets of wood separated by strips between the edges. If the door is large, an extra stiffener should be inserted to keep the panels rigid.

A simple type of closet door you can readily make consists of two sheets of quarter-inch hardboard

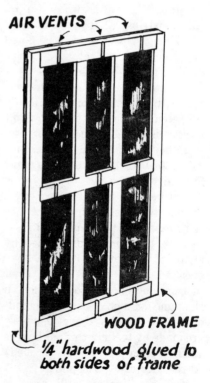

AIR VENTS

WOOD FRAME

¼" hardwood glued to both sides of frame

Fig. 24
An easy-to-make room-size door.

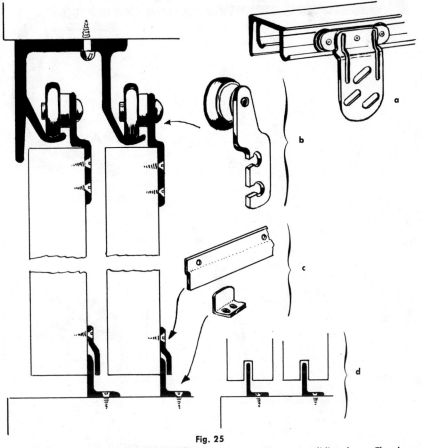

Fig. 25

For wardrobes, tall cabinets and filled-in archways you may want to use sliding doors. They hang from overhead tracks, with guides at the bottom.

glued to a 1-inch frame (Fig. 24). Because of the thin sides and large internal spaces you'll need to allow for air expansion by drilling through the frame members as the sketch shows.

Sliding Doors

Another important item, especially in connection with kitchen cabinets, is the sliding door. In the case of doors that are quite small, all you need is a pair of guides, top and bottom, well soaped or waxed. But for doors of full-sized cabinets that get a lot of opening and closing it pays to use hardware (see Fig. 25). The typical sliding-door equipment consists of a grooved track (Fig. 25a) above each door in which run the small rollers attached to the door top. The tracks,

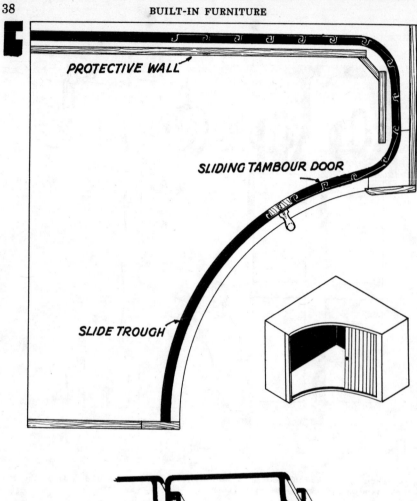

PROTECTIVE WALL

SLIDING TAMBOUR DOOR

SLIDE TROUGH

DETAIL of SLIDE (Tambour) JOINTS

Fig. 26
Metal or plastic roll-away doors are ideal for kitchen cabinets and easy to install.

single or double, are screwed to the under side of the cabinet top. A flange on the track comes down far enough to hide the top edge of the cabinet door. The rollers are attached to little brackets that screw to the inside edge of the door, and from these the door hangs (Fig. 25b). There are no rollers at the door bottom, but there is a metal strip that hooks over a guide fastened to the cupboard floor (Fig. 25c). This guide does not need to extend across the door opening and therefore can remain invisible in use.

A similar device is used for closet doors, generally with double rollers, one in line with the other. In some instances, where the door is thick enough, you can cut a groove in its bottom edge instead of at-taching a guide strip to the side (Fig. 25d).

Sliding doors of the above type are not usually made to go around corners. Instead you can buy flexible rolling doors made of interlocking strips of either plastic or aluminum. These doors come with wood-grain finishes, and they're very easy to install. They enable you to close cabinets that have curved or rounded fronts. The views in Fig. 26 show both the construction and application. All these doors need is a track cut into or formed on the wood base and top, or sides, of the cabinet, and well waxed with paraffin. This type of door can be used for living-room built-ins (standing wall cabinets, etc.) large or small. They are ideal where there is no room for swinging or rigid sliding doors.

CHAPTER 4

Construction Details for Typical Built-In Units

IN the previous chapters we have dwelt on the fundamentals of cabinet construction and the materials and devices available. Now we can turn our attention to the actual details involved in the planning and making of typical built-in pieces, both attached and free-standing. Figures 27 through 32 demonstrate the simplicity of much of this work and the routines that need to be followed.

Bathroom Medicine Chest and Dresser

This built-in (Fig. 27) is primarily a bathroom medicine chest, with a shelf that serves as a dresser with a mirror hung over it. This can go over a toilet tank or in any odd corner. It can be fastened together entirely with nails, although waterproof glue would make it more rigid.

When you have pieces of this sort, made up of shelves and divisions at right angles to one another, rigidity is lacking. You can stiffen the whole structure by attaching a thin ($\frac{1}{8}$-inch) back, which is recommended in this case.

In making this unit, the first thing to decide is how it is to be attached to the wall. If the wall studs are 16 inches apart, center to center, and in the right position, you can perhaps fit the unit to them. One good method would be to screw a strip of wood 2 inches wide to the studs and mount the unit on that. The strip would fit under the long bottom shelf between the brackets. You can use brass or iron hangers or angles screwed to the top or bottom of the cabinet and to the studs. If you can't strike a stud, you can either nail into wall plugs or use toggle bolts (see Figs. 7 and 8, pp. 22 and 23).

This type of unit — unlike some others — is best made and assembled before being put in place. The two ends of the cabinet, the partition within the cabinet, and the base are cut and put together first. If the box has a thin plywood back, cutting the back per-

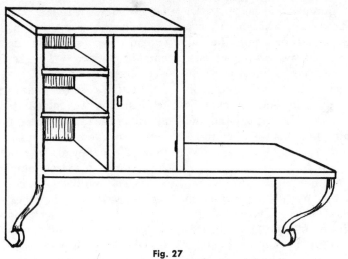

Fig. 27
Combination medicine chest and dresser for bathroom.

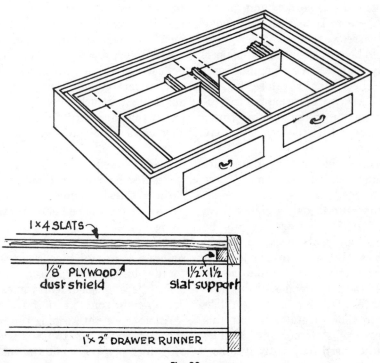

1 × 4 SLATS

⅛" PLYWOOD
dust shield

1½"×1½
slat support

1"× 2" DRAWER RUNNER

Fig. 28
Bed base with drawers.

fectly square will help square everything else. The shelves can be held by nails or screws through the sides, and the top put on last. Finally, the door is hung, after being fitted with a knob and ball-catch, and the end bracket is screwed on. It is best to sand and finish a unit of this type before installation.

Bed Base

This bed base is illustrated in Fig. 28. Here you have a simple wood frame of 1x10 pine boards inside which 1½x1½-inch strips form a ledge to receive the mattress slats. You can greatly strengthen the frame by inserting short lengths of 2x2 into the corners and fastening the boards to them with glue and screws. These 2x2 pieces should help to keep the frame positively square. You should carefully check for this before the glue sets. A strip of wood nailed diagonally across the squared frame will keep it that way while you are working on it.

In one side of this frame are openings for two drawers. These can be made in the same manner as the frame, or as detailed in Chapter 3. If they are to be opened rarely, about once a season, they can be made in the form of box trays, with the bottom merely nailed to the underside of the sides and back. They will be more difficult to slide in and out, but this may not be so important. If they are to be used frequently it is better to make them as actual drawers. In this case the sides will extend down to rest on the slides, and the bottom will be set up to clear them.

In either case the slides will extend all the way across the bed, although the drawers need not. In fact the drawers will be much easier to handle if they are no more than 3 feet long. If extra storage space is needed, another pair of drawers can be inserted in the other side of the bed to run on the same slides. In any case the slides must have raised sides (called guides) to keep the drawers exactly square with the sides of the bed.

To prevent dust from getting into the drawers they need to be closely covered with sheets of ⅛-inch plywood, as you see in the detail drawing, Fig. 28. These can be fastened at both ends under the slat support. In addition it may be advisable to attach a canvas covering to the back end of the drawer. This can be tucked in around the drawer contents each time the drawer is closed.

Besides having tight and rigid corners, the slat supports are best carried across the bed ends as stiffening and secured throughout their lengths with glue and No. 10 screws. A pair of blocks screwed to the drawer slides, after everything else is finished, will stop each drawer from going in too far.

Another way of keeping the bed absolutely square is to use a sheet of ¼-inch plywood to fill the entire space below the slat supports. If this sheet is square to begin with and fits snugly, the bed sides cannot move in relation to it. For a bed more than 4 feet wide, you would probably need to insert this plywood in two sections, but that should not affect the rigidity.

Workshop Tool or First-Aid Cabinet

In Fig. 29 is a tool or first-aid cabinet suitable for the garage or workshop. The two ends are made wider than the top and bottom so that they will act as supports when the unit is nailed to the wall studs or ceiling posts. And, as you see in the sketch, the top and bottom are set in so that the doors will be flush with the front edges of the side pieces. Remember to measure accurately. The top and bottom boards must be equal and their ends absolutely square.

This cabinet has a back which should be made first and checked carefully against the posts. You can then use the back as a guide for cutting the top, bottom and sides, and also the shelf if you decide to have one. The back will then fit between the top board and the bottom board, both of which can be nailed to it.

Floor Storage Box

A little more ambitious than the foregoing is the storage chest for outdoor cushions, folding chairs, etc., shown in Fig. 30. Its front supports a hinged table for sorting

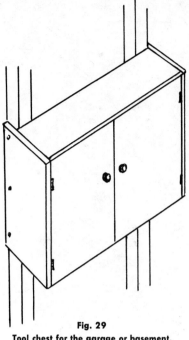

Fig. 29
Tool chest for the garage or basement.

purposes. The chest is nothing but a large box attached to the floor. Being several feet long, its cover is divided into two sections. Each lid has an adjustable, hinged wooden leg whose lower end rests in slots or notches formed by strips of wood nailed to the box end as depicted in the detail sketches.

The box is made by nailing the front (and back, if any) to the sides, and to the baseboard if there is one. If the box is built in the angle of floor and wall with no separate back or base, you will need a 2x3-inch frame instead — three pieces of 2x3 for the front and sides and one piece to support a 3-inch-wide board to which the cover

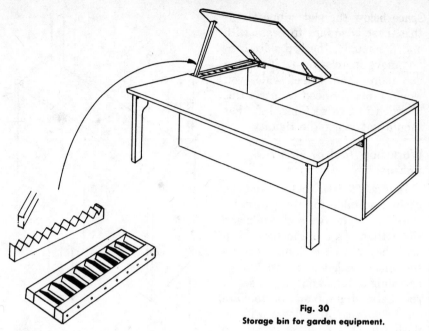

Fig. 30
Storage bin for garden equipment.

hinges will be screwed. T-hinges are used for the lids.

The table portion is hinged to the front of the box, level with the closed lids. Its legs also are hinged to the underside of the top. When they are folded up, the top hangs down against the front of the box. The legs, of course, will hold the top away from the box slightly. To eliminate this ugly feature, you will need to hinge the top an inch or so away from the front edges of the lids. This involves fastening a strip, say 1x2, along the top edge of the front board and screwing the hinges to that. If preferred, a pair of hooks can substitute for the hinges. Then the counter can be removed for storage or perhaps laid on top of the chest.

If you use boards to make sides of a box of this type, the grain must run horizontally so you will not have to fasten the lids to raw end grain. The lid grain likewise should run laterally, the end grain appearing at the sides where it will be least noticeable. The lids must be cut accurately and quite square so that the joint between them is close and neat. If plywood is used, stronger box joints will result from using square or triangular corner pieces into which the screws can be driven through the faces of the boards. Do not screw or nail into the edge of plywood.

Garage or Basement Cupboard

The next example of simple construction (Fig. 31) is a light cupboard for the garage, potting shed or basement. This unit has a ¼-inch-thick back, 1-inch board sides, and doors of 3/16-inch hardboard on light wooden frames.

The base of the cupboard is made of four pieces of 2x3 set on edge to form a rectangle and spiked together. The front and back pieces extend the full length of the cabinet floor. The floor is a 1x10 board nailed on top of the 2x3 frame. The 1x10 boards forming the cabinet sides are cut to length, the full overall height of the finished cabinet. These side boards are nailed to the ends of the base and are tied together at their upper ends by a 1x10 that forms the cabinet top. This top board should be the same length as the board that forms the top of the base.

A piece of 1x4 is now cut to the overall width of the cabinet — i.e., the width of the top plus the thickness of both side boards. This is nailed to the front of the cabinet top and to the edges of the side boards, holding the structure square. A 1x3 strip the same length as the 1x4 is now nailed to the front of the base. On top of this a length of 1x3 is run up the front edge of each side board. These strips, the vertical stiles to which the doors will be hinged, are also nailed into the front edge of the bottom board forming the cabi-

net floor. At the top they are toe-nailed into the bottom edge of the 1x4.

The two shelves are now made and inserted. These consist of 1x10 boards with a strip of 1x2 screwed to the underside of the front edge. This acts as a stiffener. After the shelves are slid in from the back on their 1x2 supports which are screwed to the cabinet ends, the stiffeners are screwed to the 1x3 door stiles (see shelf detail, Fig. 31).

The ¼-inch hardboard back, cut exactly square and to size, is now installed. This is nailed or screwed to the back of the base and to the rear edges of the sides and top. It can also be fastened to the back edges of the shelves to assure

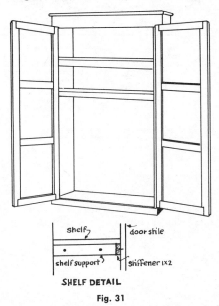

SHELF DETAIL

Fig. 31

Garage or basement storage cabinet for tools and supplies.

greater rigidity and to prevent the back from bulging when the wood shrinks. To give a finished effect, ¾-inch molding may be applied to the front and sides of the cabinet top.

After construction the cabinet can be moved into position and anchored through the top to ceiling joists, toenailed to a wooden floor, or anchored at the back with angle irons fastened to the sides. If you build the unit in position, anchor the base 2x3s to the floor, and the top to the ceiling or spacers. If no top is required, a 2x3 frame can be substituted. If you want to omit the back panel, the cabinet sides should be nailed to a pair of 2x3 or 2x4 uprights fastened to a masonry or plaster wall.

Sink and Counter for Potting Shed

Finally, in this preliminary series, we have the potting shed sink and counter (Fig. 32). This unit is entirely built into the available

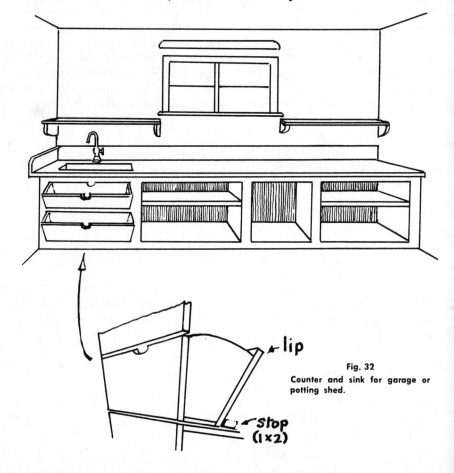

Fig. 32
Counter and sink for garage or potting shed.

space and consequently involves somewhat more complicated operations than the pieces described thus far. But it is much less difficult to construct than it may appear at first.

A frame of 2x3s on the floor forms a nailing base for the bottom of the unit and for the board frame that forms the front. If the floor is of concrete this frame should be nailed to wooden plugs driven into holes in the floor, or it may be nailed to the walls.

A 1x3 base strip is nailed to the front of the 2x3. The 1x3 vertical members of the front are doweled into the base strip, and the top strip, in turn, is doweled to the upper edges. Behind this upper section are strips of 1x3 nailed to the walls at the rear and ends. These form the anchorage for the counter top. The top is held still more securely in position by the vertical splash board at one end and at the back. However, before the top is fastened in place, the lower partitions are installed. These are of ¾-inch plywood, nailed into through the front vertical strips and, later, secured by nailing into their top edges through the counter top.

The shelves are installed along with the dividers, but these are best supported by bracket strips screwed to the end wall and partitions. The unit at the left end is a pair of tilting bins for peat moss, etc. These are merely set on shelves so that when pulled forward they can be tilted. The retaining lip, shown in Fig. 32, prevents their falling out. On the other hand, by lifting the front of the bin slightly, the whole thing can be removed. The top bin is set in low enough and is sufficiently shallow from back to front to clear the sink trap and the bottom of the sink itself. The 1x2 stop indicated in the drawing is nailed to the back of each shelf to prevent the user from pushing the bins too far in.

Where you have a sink set in a counter top such as this it is usually best to make the top out of a single sheet of plywood. The method of installing the sink will depend on the style and type of flange and anchors you buy. Although the counter shown is intended to be covered with linoleum or some other such waterproof material, the entire area around the sink can be covered instead with sheet copper or zinc held down with small nails all around the rim. Asphalt paint or some similar material under the metal will make the area waterproof.

Window Dressing-Table and Shelf Unit

Problems somewhat different from the foregoing are involved in making up a dressing-table-shelf unit such as that in Fig. 33. Here you have a combination of closed and open shelves flanking a window from the top of which they are hung. At the bottom they are connected by a counter whose center portion serves as a dressing table.

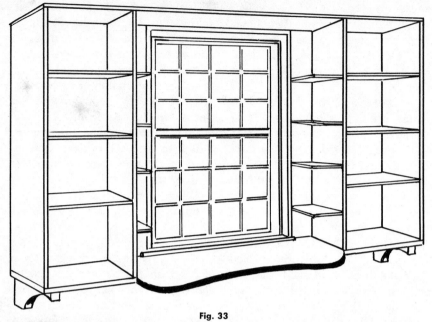

Fig. 33

This bracket-type dressing table is much simpler to make than it may appear. It fits around the window frame and is fastened to it, top, bottom and sides.

In some instances this unit could be hung almost entirely from the window frame. A large and heavy piece, however, such as the one shown, will need the further sup-

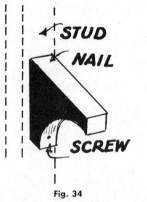

Fig. 34

Two heavy brackets like this, screwed to wall studs, support the unit at each end.

port of brackets attached to the wall studs (see Fig. 34). In any case the upper part of the shelf sections should be pulled firmly to the wall, either with screws and metal eyes driven into the studs, or by screws through a wooden back strip. Toenailing through the back edge of the end boards is not recommended; it makes an awful mess of the plaster and does not do a reliable job.

This unit can be built and mounted in one of several ways. The window is flanked by a pair of spacing boards (Fig. 35) that provide ample window clearance and permit plenty of light to enter the room. If the little corner shelves

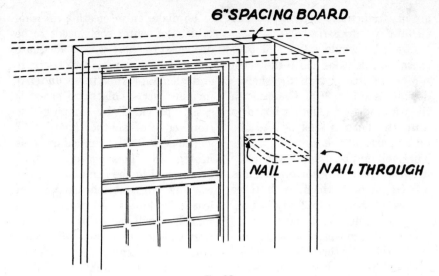

6"SPACING BOARD

NAIL   **NAIL THROUGH**

Fig. 35
Put spacing boards at each side of window to provide clearance.

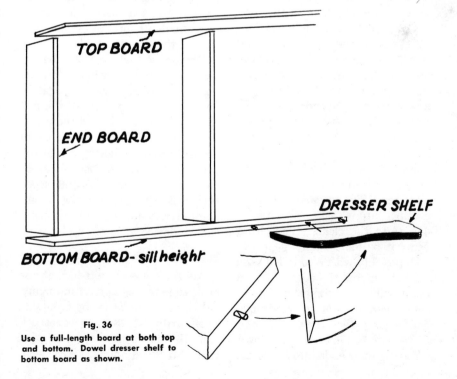

TOP BOARD

END BOARD

DRESSER SHELF

BOTTOM BOARD- sill height

Fig. 36
Use a full-length board at both top
and bottom. Dowel dresser shelf to
bottom board as shown.

are omitted, there is room for side curtains or draperies.

Over the window top and over these boards goes the full-length top board from which the shelves depend (see Fig. 36). Underneath the window goes a similar board to form the bottom shelves and the main part of the dressing table. The shelf end boards run vertically between these two horizontals and are fastened to them, with three screws at both top and bottom. Glue also helps to stiffen them.

Some of the weight of the structure is taken by the pair of brackets fastened to the wall studs below the bottom board. That is the reason for the full-length horizontal board extending *under* the end boards instead of terminating inside them. If the unit is small and no brackets are used, the vertical end boards should be an inch longer, with screws driven through their sides into the ends of the bottom board. A stronger job, of course, would result from adding cleats across the ends of the end boards, forming rabbets on which the ends of the horizontal board would rest. The screws would then go up through the horizontal board into the cleats. The cleats need not be more than 1½ inches wide, possibly with a rounded nose and a chamfered top edge. A third and possibly a simpler variation, though perhaps not so handsome, would be to extend the vertical end boards 8 or 10 inches farther down and shape their ends into brackets.

To make an interesting dressing table, the center shelf needs to be deepened so there will be adequate space for a mirror and toilet articles and plenty of knee room under it for the user. This extra space is easily provided by shaping the front edge of another board to a gentle curve with rounded ends, as in Fig. 36. This board can then be doweled to the front edge of the existing horizontal board with at least four dowels. A properly glued joint here will make this center section sufficiently solid and strong. However, it could be made to withstand considerable weight by adding another pair of brackets, one under each end of the center section and extending out almost the full depth of the curved portion of the dressing table.

Obviously this unit can be assembled over the window frame, board by board, or made separately and mounted as a unit. If the latter procedure is adopted the measurements will have to be quite accurate, and it might pay to fit the vertical side spacers last. One advantage of making the unit separately is that it can be easily painted without risk of smearing the window trim or the wall.

Box-Type Seat

Another type of built-in that appeals to most beginners (and many old hands as well) is the box-seat. Such seats are easy to construct and often mark the beginning of a cozy breakfast nook. The seat

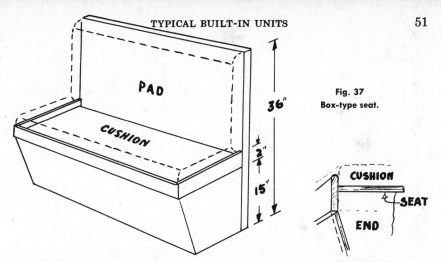

PAD

CUSHION

36"

2"

15"

Fig. 37
Box-type seat.

CUSHION

SEAT

END

shown in Fig. 37 is a simple unit consisting merely of a plywood box with a high back. The upholstery can consist of loose cushions until a special back pad and upholstered seat can be made and attached with upholstery nails.

All you need are five boards: the back, seat, two ends and a front. Theoretically, if one end of the seat goes against a wall, there should be no need for an end board there. However, an end board forms a simple means of supporting the end of the seat, and simplifies construction. The end boards should be tapered 2 inches to make heel room. When the main boards have been assembled, a low gallery of ½-inch wood, 2 or 3 inches wide, is applied to the top of the seat section to form a recess for the seat cushion. This gallery also covers the joints and gives the seat a neat finish.

If you're feeling more ambitious you can make this into a storage seat. This calls for running a 3-inch-wide strip across the back of the seat to form an attachment for the hinges. The seat board will have to extend beyond the edges of the base to rest upon them. And the cushion-retaining strip will have to be fastened to the edges of the seat. The cushion, incidentally, has to be taken off when the lid is lifted, unless the back strip is made much wider.

Dressing Unit

Here's a handy and practical built-in you'll find easy to make. This dressing unit (Fig. 38) has light plywood or wallboard construction that relies for its rigidity on its firm attachment to floor, wall and ceiling. Rigid construction is particularly necessary wherever you have doors and drawers that must close properly.

The two main units of this assembly are identical in construction, except that the doors are hinged to opposite sides. Since the material is light wallboard, hard-

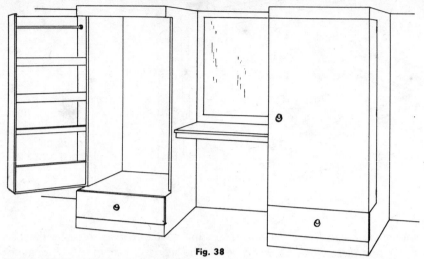

Fig. 38

Dressing table-wardrobe combination adaptable to any room. The proportions can vary widely. Both units are identical except for interior arrangements.

board or plywood, it has to be anchored firmly top and bottom. The sides and bottom therefore need to be nailed to 1x2s or heavier wood strips attached to floor and ceiling. The bases are further stiffened by the inside floor which rests on another light wood frame forming the drawer guides and slides.

It is possible to make the doors light because they are box-shaped, with deep sides that are held rigid by the series of shelves joining them. This type of door is quite useful since you can install in it such things as tie-hanging rods, handkerchief and glove trays, shirt racks, soiled-linen receptacles, and so on.

You can make a sturdy unit out of the two cupboards by tying them together with a deep-aproned shelf and mirror frame, as you see in the illustration.

Wall Niche

Going to another extreme of built-in units, Fig. 39 shows how a useful niche can be formed in an interior wall. Here all you need to do is remove a section of wallboard or plaster, on one side of the wall only, between two studs. This will open up a recess about $14\frac{3}{8}$ inches wide by $3\frac{1}{2}$ inches deep. If you skip one stud and open the next space, you will have a gap of $30\frac{3}{8}$ inches (provided the studs are spaced 16 inches on centers). In so doing you will need to remove a section of the stud in the center by cutting it $1\frac{5}{8}$ inches above and below the finished opening. Then you can insert two lengths of 2x4s horizontally and nail their ends to the studs on either side, driving an extra spike into each cut stud. (See Fig. 39b.)

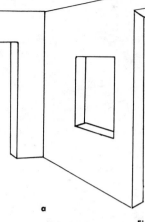
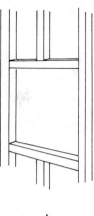

a   b

Fig. 39

An interior stud wall can be recessed for open shelves or a cupboard. Detail shows how the opening is framed with 2x4 headers.

This will give you an opening that you can trim all around with ½- or ¾-inch boards 3 or 4 inches wide. These will hide the studs. The back of the space is best hidden by a piece of plain or decorative board inserted flat against it before the trim is installed. If you're working on a plaster wall, the wall back may be too rough for this. If so, the piece of board for the back, and for the inside trim, should be nailed together first to form a box. This box then can be inserted in the hole and held in position by nailing through the trim into the studs. The job is finished by installing the trim around the hole on the room wall.

In an entrance hall such a recess may hold a mirror, and the bottom may form a shelf which can be extended outward if desired. In a bathroom the fixture could be fit-

ted with a door to form a medicine cabinet.

Adding On To Built-in Units

While all the different types of units described above are self-contained, it often happens that new

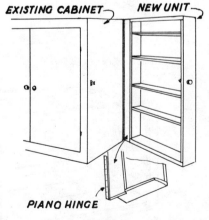

EXISTING CABINET   NEW UNIT

PIANO HINGE

Fig. 40

A unit with several applications — useful in kitchen as a spice cabinet or in bathroom as medicine chest hinged to a larger cupboard.

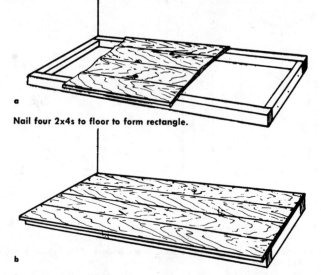

a

Nail four 2x4s to floor to form rectangle.

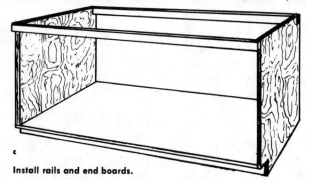

b

Cover rectangle with t&g boards, with 3-inch overhang for toe space.

c

Install rails and end boards.

d

Insert partition and door framing.

Fig. 41

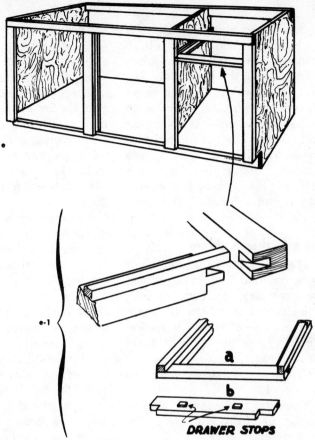

e-1

DRAWER STOPS

a

b

Install drawer slides and stops.

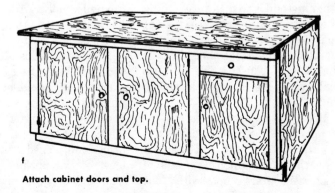

f

Attach cabinet doors and top.

Fig. 41

pieces can be conveniently attached to old ones, increasing their utility or merely using them as a support. An example of this is shown in Fig. 40. Here a wall cabinet, in either kitchen or bathroom, serves as an anchor for an additional smaller unit. Such a "door" equipped with shelves could be used as a spice shelf, as a hiding place for reserve bottles in the kitchen, or as a separate poison cabinet in the bathroom.

Basic Kitchen Cabinet

There is probably no simpler or more common built-in unit than the ordinary kitchen cabinet. Therefore we give here its details as an example of basic construction practice. The project is to build into a corner a simple floor cabinet with three cupboards and one drawer.

There are two ways of building a structure of this kind. One is to erect a solid frame — of 2x3s or 2x4s — and nail boards to it to form the sides, ends and top. The other method is to make everything of tongue-and-groove (t & g) boards or plywood sheets, eliminating the need for a frame. This is the type of construction that we shall use in the example shown in Fig. 41.

Because this unit needs no special frame, everything is done with ¾-inch plywood and 1x3 pine, except the base which is made of 2x4s. We start then with four lengths of 2x4 nailed, edge up, to the floor to form a rectangle (Fig. 41a). Since the cabinet will have a 3-inch toe space under its front edge, this rectangle must be 3 inches shallower from front to back than the finished depth of the cabinet. A 2x4 actually measures 1⅝ x 3⅝ inches, and since we need a toe space under the counter 3⅝ inches high, we set the 2x4s on edge. These are toenailed to the floor.

The next step is to cover the 2x4 rectangle with 1-inch t & g boards to form a platform on which the rest of the structure is built. We can use boards of any width — say 5 to 8 inches — and arrange to have them overhang the front 2x4 by 3 inches to give us toe space (Fig. 41b). These boards are nailed on lengthwise so that we have the edge of the front board to nail to, and to give a finished look when the doors are opened. If the base frame is long — 5 feet or more — it may pay to put another 2x4 across the center to stiffen the cabinet floor boards at that point. These boards are nailed down with common nails 2½ inches long, known as 8-penny (8d.) nails.

Now you can install the back rail that will hold the ends and partition in place at the back. This is a piece of 1x3 nailed to the wall studs through the plaster. It must be perfectly horizontal (use a spirit level) and placed 1 inch below the level of the finished counter top. The end of the counter that will fit in the wall angle can be supported either by a solid end board (Fig. 41c) or by a 1x3 strip similar to the back support. The solid end usually is better because you can use it to attach the vertical front strip (the door stile) at that point. If you use t & g boards here, they should be placed vertically and level at the top with the top of the back nailing strip. The board (or plywood sheet) next to the back will have to be notched to fit the strip and nailed to it through the top edge at an angle. Use 3-inch finishing nails here.

Next install the other end board. This will extend to the floor and will be nailed to the bottom 2x4, after notching for the back strip and the toe space (Fig. 31c). Now you can insert the partition in the same way, nailing it into the floor board at the front edge (Fig. 41d). Then you are ready for the front horizontal rail. This also can be of 1x3, nailed to the front edges of the ends and partition. Next apply the vertical strips (also 1x3) which are cut to fit under the rail so they can be nailed to the edge of the floor board.

In Fig. 41e, you will note that there are four of these vertical strips (stiles). Three are nailed to the edges of the partitions and an extra one is inserted so that the larger space at the left can be provided with two doors. This stile is toenailed through its edges into the top rail and a wider strip is fastened behind it to form rabbets against which the two doors close.

This second board can be nailed or screwed to the back of the top rail and toenailed at the bottom. The next step is to install the drawer slides. (See Figs. 41e and 41e-1.) Because of the vertical 1x3s, the drawer front opening is narrower than the space between the partition and the end board of the counter. The extra space alongside the drawer is taken up by wooden guides that rest on top of the drawer slides as you see in the sketch (a). These guides should be exactly in line with the sides of

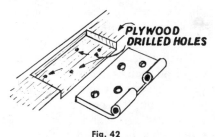

Fig. 42
A butt hinge installed flush.

the drawer opening, and square with the front. The detailed sketch shows how the slide and guide and the front cross-member that joins them are assembled. These should be screwed and glued firmly in place. To stop the drawer from being pulled completely out by accident, you can glue thin blocks to the top of the cross-member and glue another pair of blocks to the drawer bottom so that they meet when the drawer is fully opened. The making of drawers was discussed earlier, and this one can be of the simplest kind.

The cabinet doors can be single sheets of plywood, or made up from t & g boards held together with battens across the back. (See Fig. 41f.) You even can make a simple framed door from pieces of 1x3 and a ¼-inch plywood panel. The door frame joints can be half-lapped or mitered, and the frame itself either rabbeted or plain, with applied molding to hold in the panel. Surface hinges are of course the easiest to apply; all you have to do is screw them to the outside of the door and the cabinet frame. The only thing that needs watching is the hinge pin; it must be exactly over the crack between the door and frame and in line with it. Installing a butt hinge is a little more complicated but calls for more care than skill. You can use butts with thick plywood, but the screw holes should be drilled first, and fairly long screws should be used. (See Fig. 42.)

Door and drawer handles of a somewhat modern type can be made from triangular-shaped blocks of wood. They are attached by inserting a screw from the inside of the drawer front or cupboard door. Or you can buy attractive metal or wood handles that are easy to install.

After completing the counter, the whole thing should be gone over with 4/0 garnet paper to remove rough edges and surface spots. If the counter is to be covered with linoleum or plastic, this operation is best saved till last.

From what has been said above, it should be clear that, if studied in detail section by section, none of these pieces is really difficult to understand or complicated to make. The same method of analysis can be applied to the larger and more advanced projects presented with less detail in the next chapter.

CHAPTER 5

Room-By-Room
Built-Ins to Make

Series 1
KITCHEN

Combination Kitchen Cabinet

Usually, no room has greater need for built-in pieces than does the kitchen. Here you can progress from simple racks and shelves to cabinets with cupboards and drawers.

One of the commoner combinations of counter, cupboards and drawers is shown in Fig. 43. The number of units and their dimensions can be juggled to suit your own requirements.

The counter is made first, as described on page 56. In this instance, however, the right-hand end of the piece is carried up to the ceiling so that it forms one partition of the adjoining refrigerator recess and overhead storage cupboard.

As in all kitchens, the counter top should overhang the base by a couple of inches. Then, if anything is spilled it won't run down the front of the cabinet and get into the drawers or cupboards. The standard counter height is 36 inches, but it is best to regulate this to suit the person who is to use it most.

The center section below the cabinet drawers is a bin, shown in detail in Fig. 44. This is hinged at the bottom, and the sides need to be shaped to clear the opening as it is swung outward. You can check that distance with a string and pencil from the center of the hinge, as shown. By attaching a chain to the back of the bin, you can keep it from tipping too far forward when opened. Note that the bin is stiffened in the corners with quarter-round fillets. The quarter-round eliminates dust-collecting angles.

Another thing to note about this unit is the drawer separation. Here

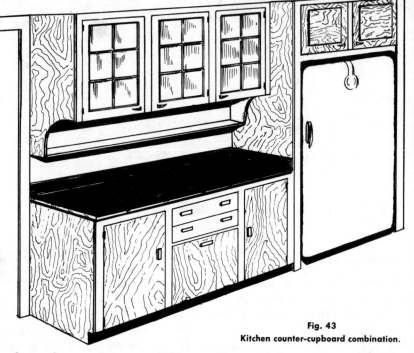

Fig. 43
Kitchen counter-cupboard combination.

you have the usual drawer slides, but the upper drawer slide is hidden by a lip formed on the front of the top drawer (Fig. 45). You can do the same with the bottom one, forming lips either top or bottom so that each drawer front covers half the spacing strip.

This counter top is finished with linoleum or plastic set in cement and held all around by metal trim. The vertical splash guard is 5 inches high.

The adjoining storage cabinets over the refrigerator are at ceiling height. But since they are supported from the floor they need no ceiling attachment. With the outer partition cut to fit snugly between ceiling and floor, all you need to hold it is a light frame (2x2 inches) under the cupboards. This is nailed to the counter end-partition and to the wall as well. The outer partition (the one at the extreme right in the illustration) is toe-nailed to the floor, or you can nail it to a 2x2 spiked to the floor. Then the facing frame is added. The horizontal members are installed first, firmly nailed to the partitions and the cross-frame.

The ceiling cabinets are typical kitchen units. They can have glazed, solid-paneled or flush-surface doors. No top is needed because the ceiling serves in that capacity. The first job, then, is to

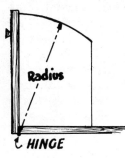

Radius

HINGE

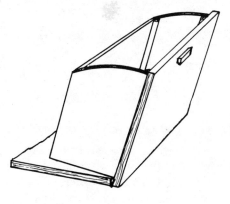

Fig. 44
Bin for counter-cupboard.

cut out the cupboard ends, partitions and bottom. Attaching the cabinet to ceiling and wall is the next step.

You can fasten a 2x3 to the ceiling as a nailer for the front of the cabinets and build them into it. A better plan, usually, is to make the cabinet unit first and then attach it. In either case, it can be held by nails through a 1x3 at the top of the back and by nails through the front into the 2x3. If the cabinet does not extend upward all the way to the ceiling (see Fig. 46), mount it first on a wall nailer, using a similar supporting strip at the bottom, either inside or outside. Fill in the space over the cabinet afterward. The filler board (fascia) can be ½-inch material nailed to the top edge of the front of the cabinet and perhaps a piece of molding put in the angle.

Glass doors are not difficult to make. Buy lengths of muntin, and fit them vertically into square mortises cut in the rails (see Fig. 71b, p. 79). Mortise the muntins where they join one another at right angles. The rail material also can be bought, and you can cut to suit with either square or mitered joints (Fig. 19), doweled, or glued and nailed. Keeping both the frame and the muntins exactly square is the major problem here. A rectangle of scrap lumber nailed

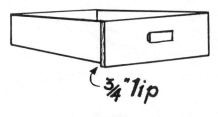

¾" lip

Fig. 45
Lips on drawer fronts hide slides and spacing strips between drawers.

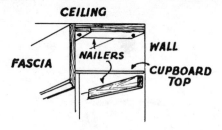

Fig. 46
Method of attaching cabinet to wall and ceiling.

that it will receive the door frame snugly and exactly. Fit the frame into it while you mark out the mortises for the muntins.

Sink Cabinet and Counter

In many kitchens, the sink counter is separated from a breakfast nook by a narrow serving counter at right angles to the main one as in Fig. 47. These counters are made as a unit with the tops level all around. The projecting counter is basically a cupboard with a set

to the bench or floor can be a great help. See that the rectangle has accurate 90-degree corners and

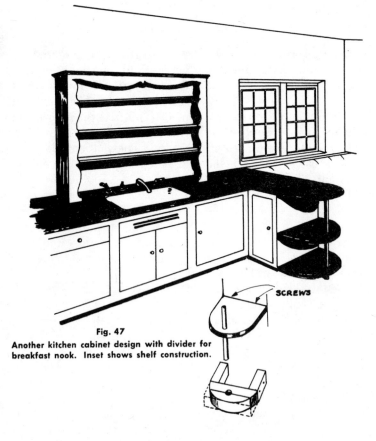

Fig. 47
Another kitchen cabinet design with divider for breakfast nook. Inset shows shelf construction.

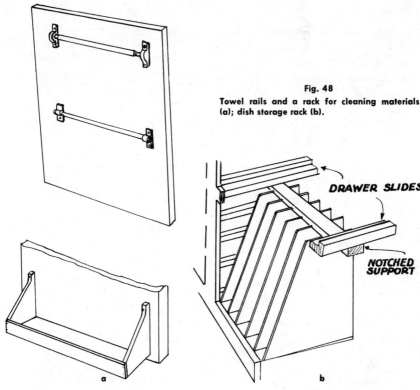

Fig. 48

Towel rails and a rack for cleaning materials (a); dish storage rack (b).

DRAWER SLIDES

NOTCHED SUPPORT

a

b

of round-ended shelves attached. The shelf construction is shown in detail in the inset. Plywood (¾-inch) is used for the cabinet doors, partitions and ends. The rest is 1-inch pine, and the finish is a stain, but paint can be used. Apart from the 2x4s in the base, and stiffeners at the sink end, no framing is used. The ventilation holes in the front sink board are easily made with a circular saw. You can make slightly wider ones with a hand saw (starting with a drilled hole, then a keyhole saw), if you prefer. Otherwise you can substitute a row of drilled holes.

The large doors are equipped with rails for towels and a rack for cleaning materials (Fig. 48a). If desired, one cupboard can be fitted with racks, as you see in Fig. 48b, for trays or china. The ⅛-inch plywood or hardboard partitions are held in saw cuts in the top strip, and between ¾x2-inch spacers at the bottom.

Plastic counter tops are easily laid (to maker's instructions), and the sink is installed either below or flush with the top. The detailed sketches (Figs. 49a and 49b) show both methods of installation.

Stove Cabinet

Alongside the kitchen stove an efficient arrangement calls for storage facilities for pans and pan lids, for cake and bread tins and for other cooking utensils and implements. In the drawing, Fig. 50, the compact design of storage units is

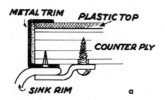

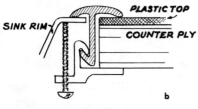

Fig. 49

Two methods of installing sinks with standard fixtures.

given interest by the use of striated plywood. The cabinets flanking the copper hood (which incorporates a fan and a fluorescent light) store dishes, coffee percolator, tea pot and similar items. At the immediate left of the stove is a sliding-shelf unit which greatly economizes the space needed for pans. Figs. 51 and 52 show construction details of these storage units.

To keep the front from dropping

as the shelf unit is pulled out, a 3-inch rubber wheel is attached to the bottom board (Fig. 51a). The whole unit is kept in position by the 3-inch-wide wooden slide under the base (Fig. 51b). This slide works in the guides that you see in Fig. 51c.

Another innovation is a set of sliding trays that form storage shelves for pan lids, cake tins and other cooking utensils. As you see in the drawing (Fig. 52a), these drawers are even simpler to make than regular drawers. The entire opening is covered by a door. Note that the ends of the guides have to be set far enough back in the cabinet to allow the tray fronts to fit behind the closed door (Fig. 52b). For smooth operation the slides and guides should be heavily waxed with paraffin.

Housekeeper's Desk

Fig. 53 is a simple desk with eight file and storage drawers and a concealed drawer in the desk top. The accessories consist of a ceiling light, electric outlets for desk lamp and radio; and a baize- or cork-covered board for notes and menus. The ceiling cabinets have two shelves apiece for cookbooks and other reference material.

The construction of this unit is simplified by making the two sets of drawers separately. The one that fits into the wall angle needs no side next to the wall, and neither one has a back. They can be fastened to the floor through the 2x4

Fig. 50
Kitchen cabinets made with striated plywood and incorporating sliding trays and pan rack.

a

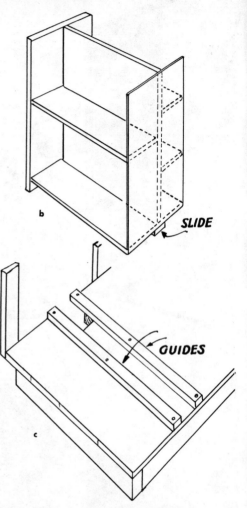

b

SLIDE

GUIDES

Fig. 51
Sliding shelf unit for pans.

c

frames that form their bases and further held in position by the counter which is screwed to 1x2 cleats fastened to their sides.

To get the flush-front effect, you can make the top overhang the thickness of the front stiles with the grain running lengthwise. If you use plywood here, the edge should be covered as described

earlier, or you can set the top behind the front, as detailed in Fig. 54.

Note that the desk section has a deep apron (4 inches or so), with a matching drawer in the middle. The front of the drawer extends below its bottom about 1/4 inch so that it can be opened without a knob. Make the apron joints care-

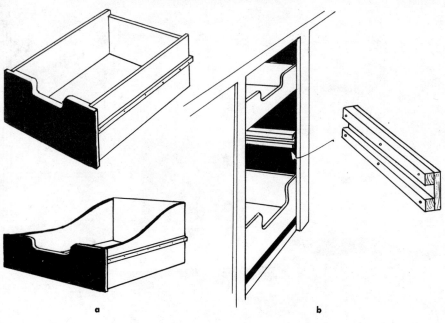

Fig. 52
Storage drawers for cooking utensils.

fully so the drawer will not be noticeable. This drawer runs on slides (see Fig. 55). The two top drawers in the side units are made without a visible separating bar by extending the upper drawer front downward (Fig. 56) to cover the bar which is set back behind the front stiles.

Back-of-Door Racks

In the kitchen there are always possibilities for adding conveniences, and many of them call for no great effort or designing ability. Fig. 57, for example, shows a simple rack designed to hang on the back of a door. This will hold anything from pan lids to potatoes. You can

use three or four of these on one door, one above the other.

Divided Shelves

Shelves with racks — vertical or horizontal — are useful for stacking items such as trays, dishes, lids and other equipment so that one piece can be removed without disturbing the rest. A simple type of vertical-storage rack is shown in Fig. 58. The vertical dividers can be cut back to make it easier to grasp the object, and the shape of the front edge given a decorative curve. The professional method of attaching dividers is to set them in slots (dadoes) cut into the top and bottom boards. A simpler way is

Fig. 53
Housekeeper's desk.

to nail into them through the boards, or hold them with either narrow strips (cleats) or boards of the full width of the space. In the latter case you can use 1x2s for the top and bottom boards.

Bread Board or Pull-Out Shelf

Another useful accessory is the pull-out shelf or bread board. This takes up very little room under the counter top, as you see in Fig. 59. The board preferably should be made of maple and fitted with a stop at the back end to prevent it from tilting when pulled all the way forward. Instead of making a dummy drawer of it to match other drawers, as shown, you can attach a knob directly to the board and make the opening that much shallower.

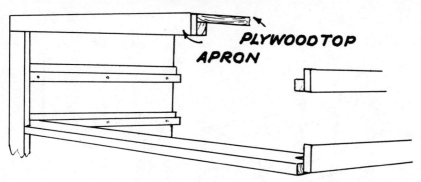

PLYWOOD TOP
APRON

Fig. 54
For flush-front effect, make top big enough to overhang stiles.

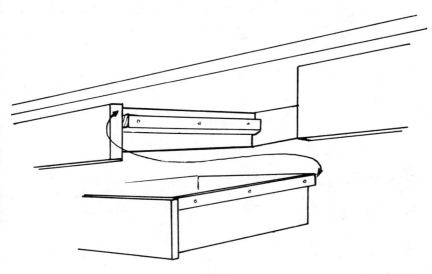

Fig. 55
Drawer slide construction.

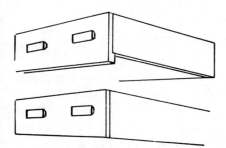

Fig. 56
Make top-drawer front overhang and ob-
scure separating bar.

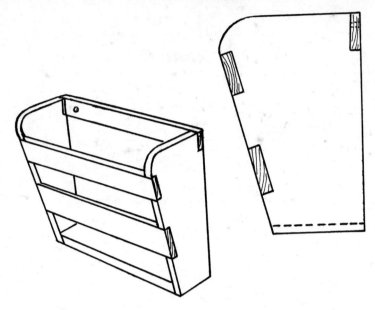

Fig. 57
Simple rack to hang on back of door.

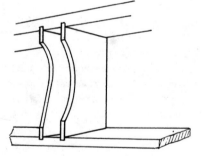

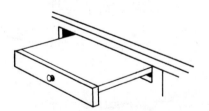

◄   **Fig. 58**
Vertical storage rack.

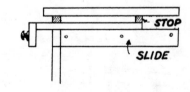

SPACER   CLEATS

Λ   **Fig. 59**
Pull-out bread board.

Ironing-Board Storage

A handy and unusual method of storing the ironing board is shown in Fig. 60. To stow it you merely fold up the legs and swing the whole thing into the counter as in the sketches. You can make a neater job by covering the opening with a lid that lets down. This makes the opening dust-tight, and it looks like a drawer.

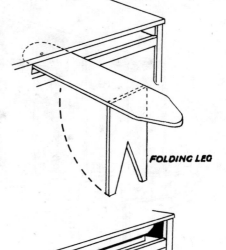

FOLDING LEG

Fig. 60
Ironing board storage.

Series 2
DINING ROOM

Partition Cabinetwork

Where you have a dining room separated only by a partition from the kitchen, you have a wonderful opportunity for the exercise of ingenuity. You can install either a very simple or a very elaborate partition with provision for opening or closing part of it and for building in storage space in either or both sides of it.

Fig. 61 is the kitchen side of a partition which can include shelves or cupboards above and drawers and cupboards below. In the example shown, the back of the shelves is made of a translucent, corrugated plastic, resembling

glass, that can be sawed and nailed. The end three feet of this back forms a drop table (Fig. 62) that lets down into the dining area. The legs swing down as the table section is lowered. The back of this drop section can be covered with striated plywood and painted a light green to give some feeling of continuity with the plastic. Obviously, the partition can be kept low as in Fig. 62 or carried up to the ceiling as in Fig. 61.

Wall Box

A far less imposing but very useful and decorative piece is the wall

72

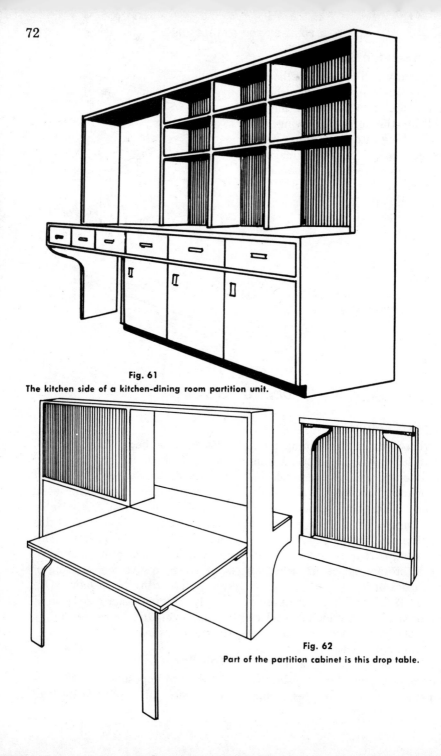

Fig. 61
The kitchen side of a kitchen-dining room partition unit.

Fig. 62
Part of the partition cabinet is this drop table.

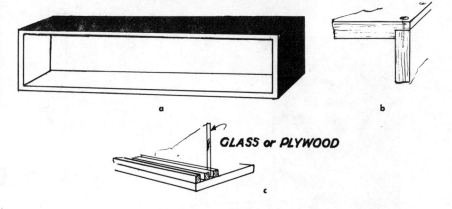

a

b

GLASS or PLYWOOD

c

Fig. 63
This wall box can also serve as a sideboard.

box shown in Fig. 63a. The box actually can serve as a sideboard, the top forming a shelf for display pieces while the interior is used for silver storage or for china.

In its simplest form this box is made with a substantial back that is screwed to the wall studs. The top is rabbeted to cover the top edge of the back, as you see in Fig. 63b, and to stiffen the whole structure. The ends are set inside the top and bottom. If desired, sliding doors of glass, plastic or plywood can be fitted with ¼ x ¼ strips forming top and bottom guides (Fig. 63c). This entire piece should be heavily lacquered or covered with a plastic film.

Apartment-Type Dining Unit

In small rooms and apartments, a dual-purpose built-in that looks like a portable piece of furniture may be of particular interest. The example shown in Fig. 64a can have

either a plain front, or panels can be applied to make the unit look like a highboy (Fig. 64b). Also, the lower part can be made as a cupboard instead of drawers.

This unit is best made in two sections, each firmly attached to the wall through the back. With the body unit made rigid in this way, the large drop-front pictured in Fig. 64a can be adequately supported on a single, detachable leg. This leg is cut square, with a slight taper. The top end, which fits snugly in a drilled hole, is rounded.

The body of the drop-front is made of a sheet of ¾-inch plywood banded with strips of any good wood such as maple, mahogany or fruitwood to form a neat and decorative edging. The panels, if used, should be of the same decorative wood, ¼-inch thick and applied with brads and glue. (See Fig. 65.)

The plywood surface (the top

Fig. 64

Combination luncheon table and dinnerware storage cabinet disguised as a tall chest. Can be made with dummy drawer front.

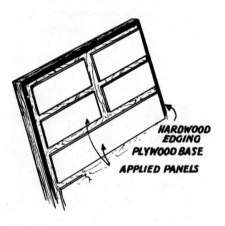

HARDWOOD EDGING
PLYWOOD BASE
APPLIED PANELS

Fig. 65

Cabinet panels are glued and bradded on.

METAL HOLE COVER
SOCKET HOLE

28"

Fig. 66

The cabinet's table leg. Socket hole is covered with bedpost ornament.

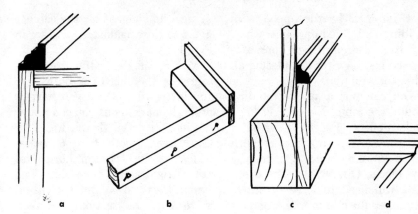

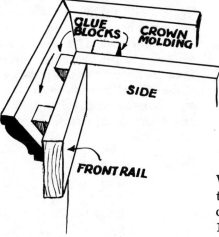

Fig. 67
Decorative moldings, base construction and cornice.

when the table is down) should be heavily lacquered or sanded smooth and covered with a plastic film before banding. A socket hole for the leg, at least 1 inch in diameter, should be drilled through a drawer panel and well into the plywood, so that you have ¾ or ⅞ of an inch to hold the leg rigid (see Fig. 66).

When not in use, the leg goes inside the cabinet bottom, and the hole is covered with a bedpost ornament 1½ inches in diameter. You can get this from any cabinet-hardware store or supplier.

The lower chest is topped with a gallery made of an ogee molding or quarter-round molding that covers the joint between the sides, front rail and top panel (Fig. 67a). The cabinet base is made on a 2x3 frame fastened to the floor (Fig. 67b). The decorative baseboard of the cabinet, covering the front and sides, is known as the plinth. This is a 1x5-inch board topped with molding and glued on as shown in Fig. 67c. The plinth, of course, is applied last — after completing all other construction.

You can put a simple molding around the top of the cabinet for a modern effect (Fig. 67d), or build out a more imposing cornice with 4-inch crown molding supported by glue blocks (Fig. 67e). The drop-front will need to have its hinge leaves set flush into the wood as shown in Fig. 68.

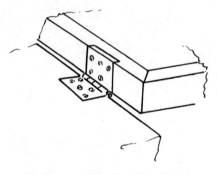

Fig. 68
Set hinges for drop-front flush into wood.

China Cabinet

A china cabinet with storage cupboards (Fig. 69a) can be built into any corner or recess, or made to flank a doorway. The base is built on 2x4s with the cabinet floor on top of them. Use ¾-inch t & g boards for the floor. Since the 2x4 is actually 1⅝ inches thick, the ¾-inch t & g board will bring it up to 2⅜ inches. Now if you use a 2-inch-wide board across the bottom at the front, you will have a

⅜-inch lip above it for the cabinet doors to close against, as you see in Fig. 69b.

Making the decorative front surrounding the shelves is both easy and interesting. Once you have it properly marked out you can follow the idea in detail sketch Fig. 69c. Use 1-inch wood, 4 to 6 inches wide, and let the top horizontal rail go right across the stiles. The simplest way to lay out the curves is to cut one section (between shelves) out of brown paper and run a piece of chalk over its edge. Cut out with a scroll saw or coping saw if you have no jig saw.

Since the ends of the shelves are covered, you can use square wood fillets to support them. Fit the top of the cabinet as close to the ceiling as possible and seal any slight gap or irregularity with ogee or cove molding.

Corner Cupboard

Fig. 70a shows a popular type of storage unit for both traditional and modern interiors. For the traditional model start with 2x4s nailed to the floor in three sections as shown in Fig. 70b. The two end pieces will be at right angles to the wall. To make a stiff job (see Fig. 70c), use vertical 2x3s against the wall and 1x4 boards in the wall angle. Insert blocks in each corner to serve as nailers for the t & g floor boards and the center shelf. Then lay the cupboard floor flush with the front faces of the 2x4s, and the shelf in line with it. Fasten the two

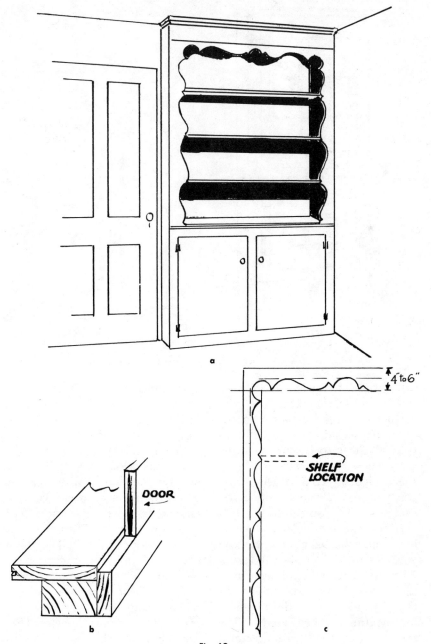

4" to 6"

SHELF LOCATION

DOOR

a

b

c

Fig. 69
China cabinet with storage cupboards.

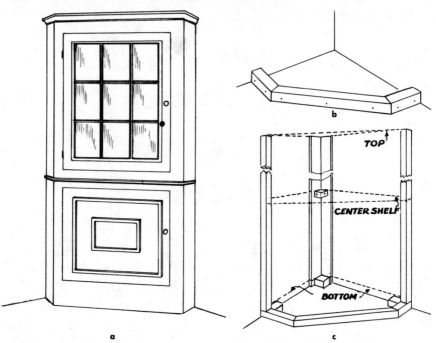

Fig. 70

A built-in corner cupboard can be made to look old-style or modern.

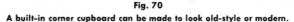

side uprights to the 2x3s. Next add the door stiles, then insert the front bottom board (also nailed to the 2x4). Note that the edges of each stile will have to be cut to 45 degrees where they meet the sides of the uprights. You will find that you can nail through this angle using 3-inch finishing nails.

If the cupboard goes to ceiling level, you will need no top. Instead you can nail a 1x3 board to the four uprights, cutting its end to fit the angle. This will serve to attach the top rail without the necessity for making tenoned joints. The top is finished off with a crown molding.

Intermediate shelves can now be cut and inserted. The upper shelf will look more interesting if the front edge is a double curve.

Finally, make the doors. The lower one, being solid, can be made of plywood faced with pine or maple (whichever wood you use for the rest) and decorated with ¼ x 1-inch strips. The upper door can be solid or glazed. The glazed door you can make, or have made for you. If you attempt it yourself, you can purchase and use regular molded glazing bars (Fig. 71a). The detail sketches (Fig. 71b) show how the glazing bars are put together. A beaded frame sec-

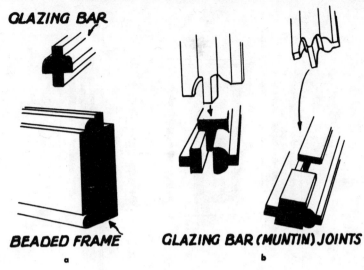

Fig. 71
Glazing bars, muntin joints and beaded frame used in glass door construction.

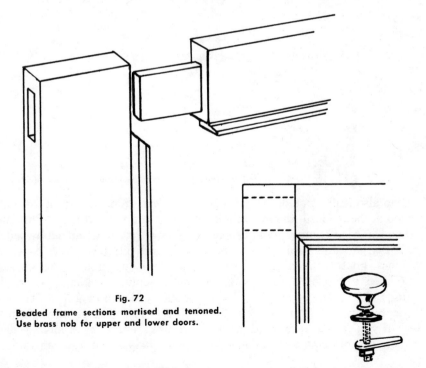

Fig. 72
Beaded frame sections mortised and tenoned.
Use brass nob for upper and lower doors.

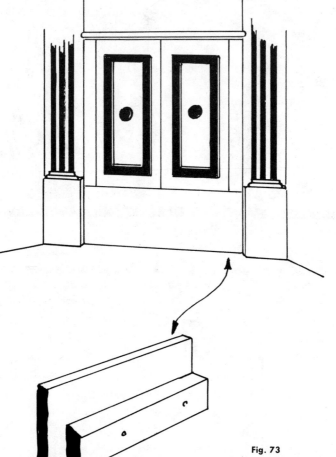

Fig. 73
Modern version of cupboard, flanked by pedestals and pilasters.

tion also is illustrated. This frame should be tenoned, the inner molding being cut through at 45 degrees as Fig. 72 shows. An old-fashioned brass knob with a finger catch (called a cupboard turn) can be used for both upper and lower doors (see Fig. 72, inset).

If you decide on the modern version of this cupboard (Fig. 73), you can run the front straight across the room corner. This produces a flat front, flanked by pedestals and pilasters. The pedestals are built up from 1-inch boards with applied moldings, as in the detailed sketch (Fig. 74). The vertical 1x6 pilasters are given a grooved effect by applying dark paint stripes. Or you can tack on

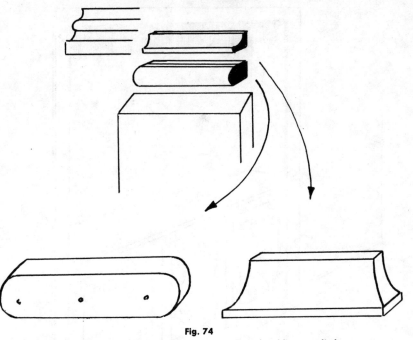

Fig. 74
Pedestals can be built up with 1-inch boards and moldings applied.

¼ x ¾-inch strips and paint them to emphasize the contrast. You will need to use a base molding that has a flat upper surface ⅜-inch deep for these ¼-inch-thick strips to stand on.

If the cupboard looks too tall or in need of more finish, you can band it horizontally at the center with a strip of nose molding (Fig. 75). This also will serve to make the cupboard look like a piece of movable furniture that comes apart in the middle.

Dining Room – Living Room Archway Fillers

One of the commonest opportunities for creating storage space

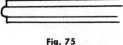

Fig. 75
Nose molding.

in living and dining rooms is provided by the wide opening that connects so many of them, especially in old houses. Here you have a space around 7 feet high and 7 or more feet wide. If there are doors from both rooms to a common hall, you may not even need a door to take the place of this opening; you can build into the entire space. On the dining-room side you may need glass and china storage, and a sideboard as in Fig. 76.

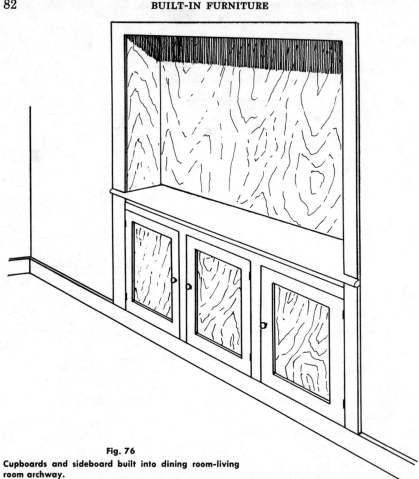

Fig. 76
Cupboards and sideboard built into dining room-living room archway.

Complete Closure by Cabinet

The first thing is to decide whether or not you want something on the living-room side of the wall also. Since this wall or partition may not be more than 5 inches thick, you will not have much to work with. However, you can put the upper recess in one wall and the lower recess in the other one. Ordinarily you will do best to work from one side only. Then you can close in the other wall entirely, using either plywood or plaster board. If you use the latter, you will need some support (such as a 2x3) for the plaster board joints. This will, of course, cut down the depth of opening available on the other side.

On the other hand, there are available proprietary boards that come in sizes large enough to cover the entire opening. These boards can be bent sufficiently to go through a normal-sized door. An alternative is to use a plywood or hardboard panel and support its center by the cupboard shelves you build behind it.

As a rule you will have to strip off the wood trim from around the opening. You can leave the wood inside the arch unless it sticks out beyond the wall surfaces. A piece of quarter-round molding or 1x1 square stuff around the inside and across the floor will form a seat for wallboard that you insert in the opening. This board should be flush with the wall in the other room. In front of this you then build cupboards, shelves or drawers, as in the picture, providing extra storage so often lacking in these rooms.

See Fig. 77. Start with a pair of cleats across each side to carry the board forming the cupboard top. Under the front edge of this top run a 1x3 or 1x4 rail to form an apron. The top ordinarily should extend beyond the apron to form a nose, with a piece of cove molding below it in the angle. Cleats at the bottom will serve as anchors for the bottom board which should be a continuation of the room's baseboard. In cases where you have a thin wall, you can steal more space by extending the cabinet a few inches into the room. It will look less bulky if only the base projects.

Door with Cabinet Each Side

Somewhat similar construction is followed where you install a door in the center of the opening (Fig. 78). Here you need to fit the door frame into the opening first, using 2x4s and applying a 1-inch pine casing to them. Behind the recess fit a sheet of pressed board, fastened to the 2x4s and to the edges

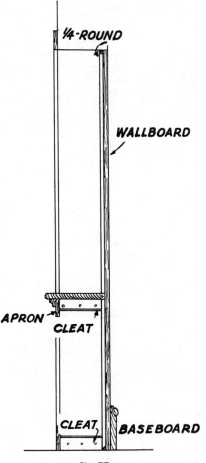

Fig. 77
Cross-section of archway opening.

Fig. 78
You can install a door in opening, flanking it with shelves and cupboards.

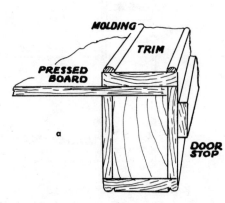
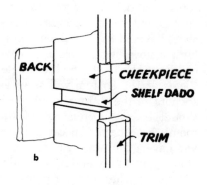

Fig. 79
Application of door trim and shelf supports.

of the archway's inside trim. Then apply the door trim as in Fig. 79a.

In front of the pressed-board partition pieces of cheap 1-inch material can be installed over the face of the original trim to form cheek pieces. By spacing these short lengths of board ¾ inch apart, dadoes are formed into which the shelves will fit (see Fig. 79b). With the shelves in position, attach the vertical trim at the edges of the opening and on either side of the door. This covers the ends of the shelf dadoes. For decoration, apply half-round molding around the edges of the shelf openings.

Below the shelves the closets are constructed in the usual way. If you need storage space in the adjoining room, you can make these closets open into that room. Then you have on the dining-room side a pair of flat surfaces that can be dressed up with panels of plywood.

Reducing Opening with Decorative Panels

In cases where the opening is shallow or where you do not need storage space, you can cut down the opening with decorative panels. These can be set out to the thickness of the walls or built inside the opening to any desired thickness.

In the example illustrated in Fig. 80, the trim is applied to the outside edges of the opening. It consists of pressed board in a light finish, given a panelled effect with ¼x1-inch lathing at the edges.

You can cover the board with wallpaper or decorative plastic, or paint a design on it. Against a dark background, this treatment can be very effective, as you see from the picture.

Fig. 80
An old, between-room opening can be converted into a decorative doorway.

Archways into Walls

Another excellent treatment for an unwanted archway or doorway is to turn it into a wall. In the wall you can have a variety of built-in conveniences and decorative devices.

First remove the opening trim, then install 2x4 studs and nail gypsum board (sheetrock) to both sides. Finish the joints with joint cement and joint tape. The result will be what is apparently a plaster wall in both rooms. But in that wall area you can have cut-out spaces of almost any size and shape, practically the full thickness of the wall. These spaces — filled with shelves, compartments with or without doors, or glass enclosures — must of course be planned for when putting up the studding.

If, for example, you want a rectangular space in the center of the new wallboard area, provide a stud frame for it. Separate the studs the width of the required opening; tie them together with horizontal pieces of 2x4. Then cut the sheetrock to fit and nail it to the studding. Inside the opening insert a wooden frame made to fit and finish it off with trim nailed around the opening so that it covers the edges of the frame 2x4s. For trim you can use molding to hold a glass pane. If you decide to put a light inside the opening you will need to allow for it when you insert the studs, installing the wiring at the same time.

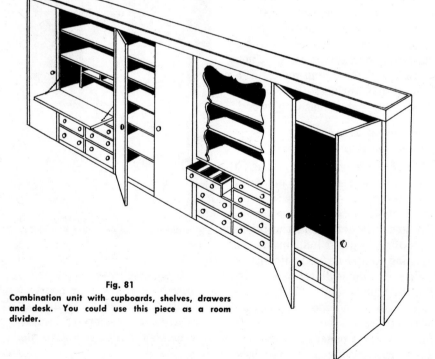

Fig. 81

Combination unit with cupboards, shelves, drawers and desk. You could use this piece as a room divider.

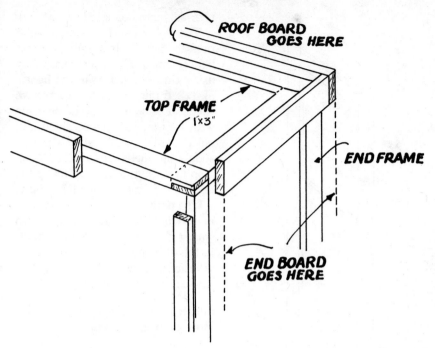

Fig. 82
Frame construction of multi-purpose unit.

Series 3
LIVING ROOM

Wall or Partitioning Multi-Purpose Unit

If you need to cover an entire wall with a combination built-in, or use something similar to divide a large room, a combined wardrobe, china cabinet, storage unit and desk may be the answer. Obviously, it is easy to lop off any section you don't need.

The structure shown in Fig. 81 is built as a unit, starting with a top frame of 1x3 pine, stiffened with cross-braces every 4 or 5 feet.

Around this goes another frame, built of 1x3s, with the boards on edge, as in Fig. 82. This forms a recess on top into which the top panel or roof board of the structure fits.

The base frame is built on 1x2¼ longitudinals with 1x2 end pieces. The longitudinals are rabbeted to take the ¼-inch floor panel. The ends and division walls are frames of 1x3 covered with a lining of thin

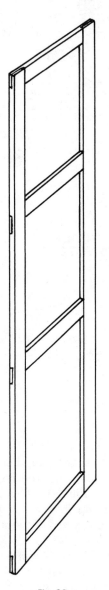

Fig. 83

Door frame made with half-lapped joints.

pressed board or similar material.

The doors can be made of solid pressed board, but you will get lighter and stiffer construction by using thin pressed board as panels in 1x3 frames rabbeted to receive them. The door frame can be made with half-lapped joints, glued and nailed (Fig. 83), and the panels should be glued and nailed to them. Another alternative is to make the doors of ¾-inch sanded Novoply.

The desk drop is made to fold up and is held in that position by a spring clip. A suggestion is made in the drawing for a baize-lined silverware drawer and for dustproof drawers under the hanging closet.

Radio, Phonograph, Record-Storage and Drawer Unit

A multi-purpose unit very much in the modern manner is shown in Fig. 84. Here you have a built-in radio-phonograph-record storage desk and a variety of drawers. The base board of this structure is carried on a single 2x4, planed smooth and stood on edge. It is also fastened to the wall but can be made free-standing by putting transverse lengths of 2x4 under it.

Attached to the ends of the base board are the vertical panels. The two inner partitions also go down to the base. These four uprights are firmly screwed to the wall through 1x1-inch strips attached to their rear edges (see Fig. 85). They are rigidly tied together with horizontal boards that form the top, the base of the upper closed

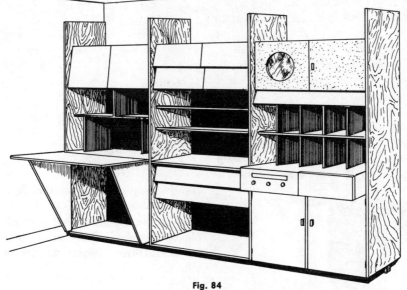

Fig. 84
A modern room divider or storage wall with desk and radio-phonograph.

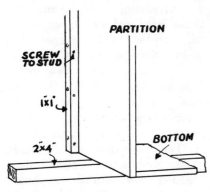

PARTITION

SCREW
TO STUD

1x1

2x4

BOTTOM

Fig. 85
Attach verticals to wall and base.

sections, and the shelves which are at differing levels.

The desk and the adjoining drawer section firmly connect the two end cells, but the phono-radio unit is differently constructed.

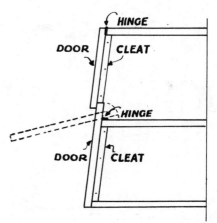

HINGE

DOOR   CLEAT

HINGE

DOOR   CLEAT

Fig. 86   ➤
Construction of sloping cupboard fronts.

The radio is mounted in a box; next to it, in a drawer, is the phonograph. This box-like frame forms a stiff support for the walls of that section and is made separately. The rest of the construction is obvious, the upper cupboards and drawers having sloping fronts. The detailed sketch, Fig. 86, shows the cupboard front construction.

The desk leaves (Fig. 87) fold inward, allowing the top to drop and cover the opening. Added at-

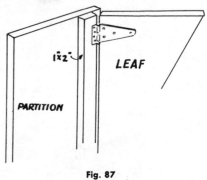

Fig. 87
Desk leaves are hinged to fold inward.

tractiveness is given to the desk pigeon-holes and record-storage rack by the use of striated or sandblasted plywood. The loudspeaker section utilizes Celotex to absorb vibration.

Simple Bookcase

In vivid contrast to the foregoing is the little bookcase shown in Fig. 88, adapted to the corner of a room. Such a built-in structure can have a "stuck-on" look unless it is handled carefully. Here the case is made part of the wall by running the baseboard and dado molding and room cornice around it. The whole thing is very simply constructed, with 2x3 floor nailers, boarded over, and the cupboard brought up to the height of the dado molding. The sketches show the construction details.

Window-Wall Storage and Display Combination

Fig. 89 is a rather ambitious treatment of a wall in which a picture-window is centered. This is

Fig. 88
Corner cupboard and bookshelf combination.

particularly useful where the ceiling is high. There are three basic units: a window seat covering a warm-air outlet, and two china display cabinets, all with small cupboards below. The whole thing is tied together with a decorative valance (Fig. 89, inset). Draperies horizontal strips let into the 2x2s to form support for the shelves. The cupboard tops are held on 2x2 frames, but the window seat calls for 2x3s or 2x4s.

The seat is divided into three sections — two for the cupboards and one for the heating duct —

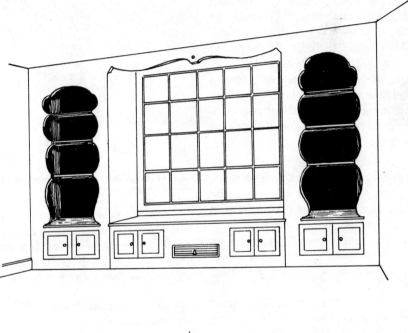

Fig. 89
Treatment for a window wall with cupboards enclosing warm-air duct.

can be hung either behind the valance or against the window frame.

The side units are of wallboard or t & g pine carried on 2x2s attached to the end walls and backing the wallboard partitions. These 2x2s are tied together with 1x1 and therefore has support at these points. The cutout fronts can be made in several pieces, the vertical boards being half-lapped or tongued-and-grooved to the horizontal ones, as in the detailed sketch Fig. 90.

TV Set and Projector-Screen Unit with Storage Space

For use either in the living room or play room, the cabinet, Fig. 91, combines several functions. In addition to providing considerable storage space, it houses a TV set and speaker and a roll-up type projection screen. The base consists of shallow and deep cupboards, the upper ones having sliding doors. Above this is the TV screen, at anywhere from 42 to 48 inches from the floor — convenient viewing heights. Above it is the speaker panel of Celotex, all capped by a covered mounting for the roll-up screen.

In use, the screen pulls down and hooks to the top of the upper cupboard. Such a unit should not be located in a corner. The set and speaker front panels are screwed to a 1x1 frame so that they can be easily removed. All joints are firmly screwed and glued to prevent vibration. The detail, Fig. 92, shows how the top of the upper cupboard (the one with the sliding doors) fits to the end boards.

The base cabinet and the upper section can be, with advantage, made as separate units, but they should be firmly joined with screws. The base cupboard embodies an idea for utilizing a deep storage space while keeping many stored items accessible. Small items go on shelves in front, bulky ones in the rear space. This entire unit is made without a frame. It consists mostly

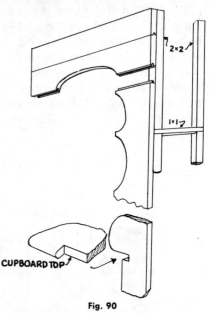

Fig. 90

Pieces of cut-out front can be attached by t&g and half-lapped joints.

of ¾-inch plywood, with sliding and hinged doors of striated plywood. If properly waxed top and bottom these small sliding doors will work without any hardware.

Free-Standing Shelf and Cabinet Built-In

This seeming contradiction in terms refers to a unit (Fig. 93) that can serve as a space divider anywhere in a room. It can be made as transparent or opaque as desired. Basically it consists of three boxes, one mounted above the other. The method of mounting gives it considerable interest, and the proportions make it attractive. Naturally the finish also adds to its appearance if done prop-

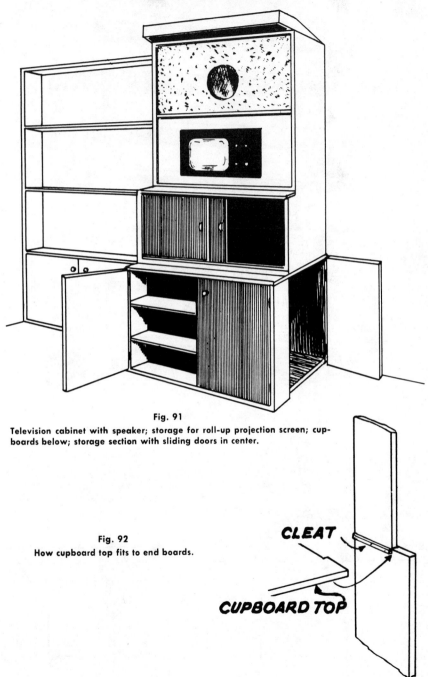

Fig. 91

Television cabinet with speaker; storage for roll-up projection screen; cupboards below; storage section with sliding doors in center.

Fig. 92

How cupboard top fits to end boards.

CLEAT

CUPBOARD TOP

Fig. 93
Simple room divider.

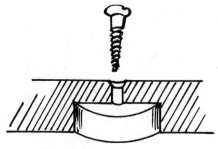

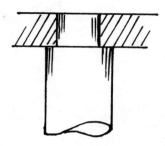

Fig. 94
Attachment of round shelf-spacers.

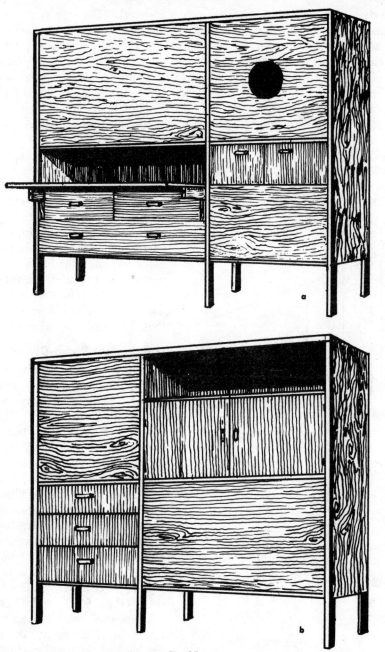

Fig. 95
Two-sided storage desk and hi-fi cabinet.

erly. Unless the box exteriors are to be covered, the joints should be mitered or half-lapped to make the end grain as inconspicuous as possible. The undersides are not so important.

The base can consist of 1x3s on edge, painted black. The lower shelf should be of at least 1-inch

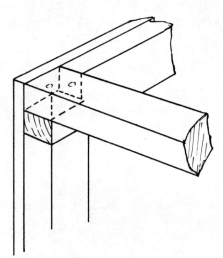

Fig. 96
Frame corner joints.

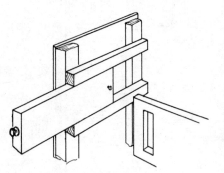

Fig. 97
Slides like this support desk flap.

material. The cabinet can have sliding doors on one or both sides. The detail sketches, Fig. 94, show alternative methods of attaching the round spacers, which should be at least 2 inches in diameter, preferably larger. They must fit tightly in their sockets exactly at right angles and be glued.

An interesting effect is secured by painting the box edges a contrasting color. If the box sides are to be covered with a plastic film, this should be applied before they are mounted. The insides of the boxes look well when painted dead black to match the base. The proportions of this unit can vary considerably, but the spaces between the boxes should always be less than the depth of the boxes.

Lightweight Room-Divider Unit

Thin plywood over a light frame makes this unit, Fig. 95, light yet strong. Make the frame first of 1x2s, nailed and glued. The corners are made as in the detail sketch, Fig. 96. Nail and glue ½-inch plywood to the ends, the top and the bottom. This forms two rectangles which can be filled in in a variety of ways.

As shown (Fig. 95a), the unit incorporates a desk, three drawers and a small cupboard in one side that could be used for a hi-fi set with speaker above it. The reverse side (Fig. 95b) embodies two drawers and two cupboards. The top drawer, a dummy, is actually the back of the small cupboard.

The desk flap can be supported by a chain or hinged support or by means of the slides shown. The construction of the slides is indicated in the detail sketch (Fig. 97). The little screw stops the slide from being pulled all the way out. The drawers are best made to run on slides, as in an earlier illustration (Fig. 18). Strips of ½-inch quarter-round will serve to seat the backs of the panels.

Series 4
BEDROOMS

Bunk Beds

This permanently installed bunk-bed unit, shown in Fig. 98, is perfectly rigid, being anchored to several wall studs. It is light in weight because boards are used instead of posts. One 4-inch and one 5-inch board, 1 inch thick, are nailed together at right angles to form the L-shaped main supports. Four of these are required, the full height of the room. Those attached to the wall (or to two walls, if in a corner) are set up first.

A pair of 1x2-inch spacers is fastened along the wall between the L-shaped supports, level with the top and bottom edges of the bunk sides. The sides are attached to these and to the corner boards. The remaining sides are screwed to the corner boards (Fig. 99a).

Strips of 1x2 are then screwed to the side boards to support the mattress laths, as you see in Fig. 99b. The same construction is followed for the storage compartment at ceiling height. The bottom of the compartment is covered in by screwing it to the supporting strips from below, after the ends have been installed. An innovation is the adjustable pillow support (Fig. 99c) — a hinged board at each bunk head held in place by dowels that fit loosely into holes in the slat supports. The ladder is made of 1x4s firmly attached at several points with screws.

Bunk Bed – Desk Combination

This bunk bed is of particular use in a boy's room (Fig. 100). It provides also a study desk with considerable storage space, plus a secret cupboard. The unit is built up of boards with no frame, although cleats are inserted in all angles where necessary, and 2x3-inch members support the bed spring or slats.

The book shelves are made shallow, with storage space behind them accessible through the inconspicuous door in the bed head. The outer edge of the door coincides with the edges of the boards, and a spring catch is fitted. The door consists of two boards held together with battens. It is made of the same boards as the bunk itself.

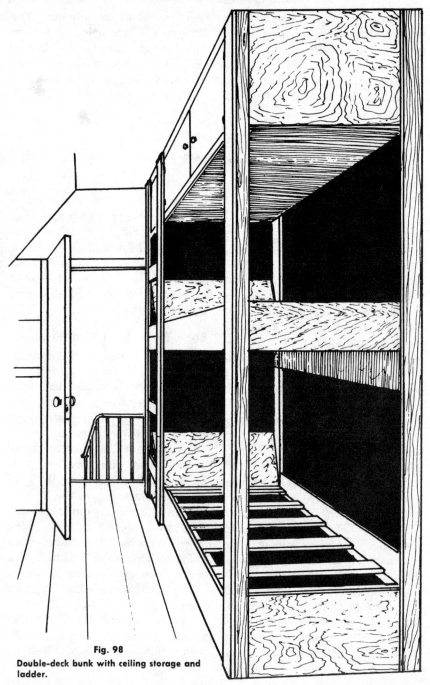

Fig. 98
Double-deck bunk with ceiling storage and
ladder.

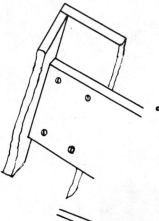

Fig. 99

Bunk sides screwed to corner boards (a); 1x2 strips
screwed to side boards to support mattress slats (b);
adjustable pillow support (c).

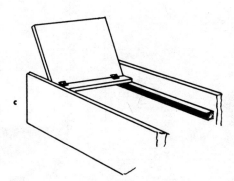

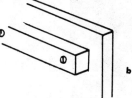

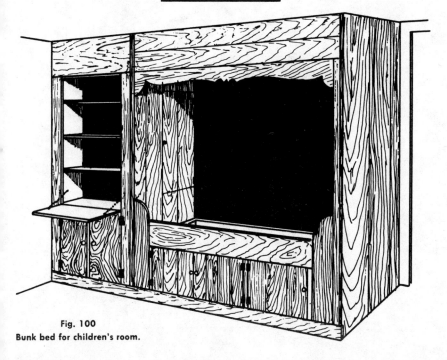

Fig. 100
Bunk bed for children's room.

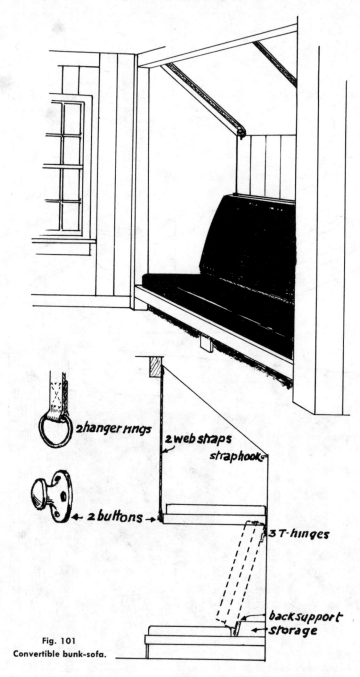

2 hanger rings

2 web straps

strap hook

2 buttons

3 T-hinges

back support storage

Fig. 101
Convertible bunk-sofa.

Below the desk is another cupboard that extends back below the secret cupboard. The desk lid can have a snap catch, thereby closing the space below the bottom shelf. The remaining construction details are obvious.

Convertible Sofa-Bunk

An excellent unit for the children's room or family game room

ance for the back, useful storage space for bed linens, etc., is made available behind it. With the upper bunk raised; it may be desirable to fit it with removable raised side pieces to keep the occupant from falling out. These can be made out of a pair of 1x10 pine or hardwood boards, each 2 feet long, for foot and head. The boards should have a pair of ½-inch dowels in the

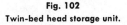

Fig. 102
Twin-bed head storage unit.

is the convertible bunk-sofa shown in Fig. 101. The back of the seat which forms the upper bunk is hinged to the wall by three — or perhaps four — strong T-hinges so that it can be raised to a horizontal position. It is held up by a pair of webbing straps attached to the ceiling or ceiling beam.

Because the lower seat-bed has to be set forward to provide clear-

lower edge to fit into holes drilled in the top edge of the upper bunk frame. The top corners of the boards should be nicely rounded off for safety's sake.

Twin-Bed Head Storage Unit

Fig. 102 is a modern twin-bed head with shelves and cupboards. Its special feature is the sloping panels which form the bed heads.

The unit should be about 10 feet long (depending on the bed width) with a 2-foot-wide center section. The base is a quadrangle of 2x4s on edge, on which the board platform is laid longitudinally.

The best method of construction is to make the platform and then

full length, with shorter pieces over the shelves. Or one piece of ¾-inch plywood, cut to fit, can be used for the entire top.

The sloping fronts are inserted last. They rest against cleats up the sides of the shelf cases and across the top and bottom. There

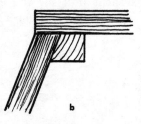

Fig. 103
The sloping fronts rest against cleats attached to shelf case sides.

erect the vertical partitions and the sloping ends on it. Since the sloping recesses for the beds have nothing behind them but a wall, there is no need to make backs for them. The three shelf sections do have backs, and these can be installed in the beginning to hold the sections in position while the top is being attached. The top is one 1-inch t & g board extending the

are two ways of making the top joint between the leaning boards and the top board, as you see in detail sketches Fig. 103a and b. It is preferable to bevel the edges of both boards to make a neat line joint, but this needs to be done quite accurately. The alternative is to run the sloping board under the top board so that the edge of the latter shows as in Fig. 103b.

Series 5
BATHROOMS

The principal requirements for a complete bathroom built-in arrangement are: dressing table, linen storage, soiled-linen disposal, storage shelves for drugs and cosmetics, drawer or cupboard for toilet articles, towel rack and a

good-sized mirror, all with adequate illumination.

General Utility Combination Built-In

The bathroom built-in illustrated in Fig. 104 fills all the requirements

Fig. 104

Bathroom built-in forms tiled bath end, towel rail and storage bin, sliding-door medicine cabinet next to mirror, and four drawers. A wooden reflector covers the fluorescent lights.

handsomely. At the head of the tub, shielded with tile, is a soiled-linen hamper incorporated in the dressing-table top. The hamper consists of a sailcloth bag on a metal rim concealed by a trapdoor in the dresser top. Behind the hamper is the towel rail. In the center is a large mirror alongside a sliding door that covers the medicine cabinet. A center drawer for toilet articles and three large drawers for linens and sundries complete the layout, which is illuminated by a series of fluorescent lamps under the running reflector.

The wall cabinets are partly recessed into the wall, projecting an inch or so over the counter. The mirror is set forward, in line with the sliding door. The two sections of the floor unit are located by the usual 2x4 nailers, with a 6-inch interval board under the three drawers. Since the drawer bottoms are all set up almost an inch from the lower edge of the drawer fronts, there is ample room for finger grip in pulling them open.

Metal or ceramic tiles are applied to the tub-end panel after construction is completed. The light-reflector can be made of wood with the under-surface heavily coated with white enamel. It is also very easy to bend a strip of thin sheet aluminum and tuck its edges inside the wood reflector

Fig. 105

A low cupboard and canopy separate the tub from the dressing area with built-in dresser drawers and cabinets.

frame. This line of lights can be confined to space over the mirror if desired.

As usual, the construction of the floor units is begun with the installation of the end boards and a light frame against the wall. The drawer slides are then inserted, and the whole structure is tied together with the top board. It will pay to complete the wall cabinets first while they are easily accessible.

Tub Separator with Canopy

Here in Fig. 105 is an effective means of adding both storage room and interest to a small bathroom. A shallow cabinet blocks off the end of the tub, and a ceiling canopy over the tub sets that area apart. The canopy is wood, with or without a lightweight roof of thin hardboard, depending on the height of the room. In a room 8 feet high or less, the valance should be attached directly to the ceiling. In an extremely high room, cabinets can be built over the valance.

The valance is easily cut out of ½-inch material with a scroll or jig saw. A large square block in the unattached corner forms a seat for the round supporting post. At the other corners smaller blocks can be used for attaching the valance to the studs.

Dresser Located at Window

In the room illustrated in Fig. 105, the window is badly placed for the best layout. It opens onto the only good spot for the dresser and

makes it necessary to use a standing vanity mirror which will not keep too much light from the rest of the room. The row of drawers fits right under the table top, supported by a 1x2 strip that runs the

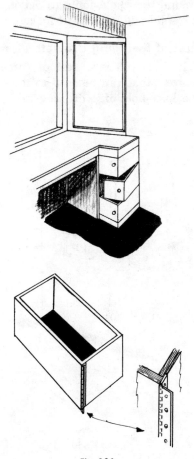

Fig. 106
Built-in dresser with stack of hinged drawers.

whole length of the dresser.

For rigidity, the stiles and drawer separators should be doweled to this strip. The cupboards are treated in the same manner, with 1x2 facings on the edges of the sides. The cupboard sides are carried down to the floor, as is the front board below the door. Then the room baseboard is carried around the whole cupboard, giving it a solid and permanent look.

Nest of Swinging Drawers

In Fig. 106 is a nest of three drawers that can be used to flank the knee-hole of a dressing table.

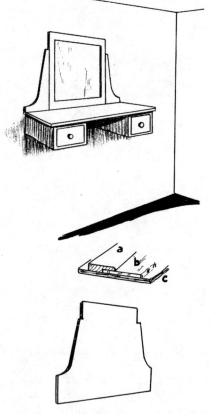

Fig. 107
Simplest form of dresser, fastened to a wall.

The end board of the dressing table will have to be carried forward the depth of the drawer along the wall for the hinge attachment. Piano-type hinges are used to carry the full weight of each drawer, but no drawer should be allowed to swing open to a point where it is not partially supported by the drawers beneath it. However, if the drawers are made large (say over 12 inches long) there should be a rigid shelf to support each one of them. This simply means separating each drawer from the next by a 1-inch board flush with the drawer fronts when they are closed.

Legless Dresser

In Fig. 107 is a simple type of legless dresser or primping table. As indicated in the detail sketches, the whole thing is mounted on a plywood backboard. This board is firmly attached to the wall studs. The drawer cases, which are made as deep as possible to act as brackets, are glued and screwed to it from the rear before mounting it on the wall. The top is then fastened in the same way to the back, and with finishing nails to the drawer sides. Then the entire unit is screwed to the wall studs through the backboard, using four screws spaced as widely ι ϳ possible in a vertical direction. Finally, the mirror is mounted as shown in the detail of Fig. 107, (a) being the molding that forms the frame, (b) the mirror and (c) the plywood back.

A variation of this unit is shown in Fig. 108. The counter and drawers are much heavier in construction and larger in dimensions. Three brackets 2 inches thick are used to support the drawers, each bracket being screwed to a separate stud. Long screws (3-inch) are used, well counterbored into the wood. The drawer unit is made separately, then mounted on the brackets by means of screws through the front and back rails.

Where further strength is re-quired, you can also screw into the studs through the back apron. This drawer assembly, of course, can be made with a solid bottom. The top is applied last and is finished with plastic film or decorative enamel resistant to alcohol and heat.

Laundry Bin and Wash-basin Counter

Fig. 109 shows a typical wash-basin fixture with a bin for soiled linen in the center. The back of

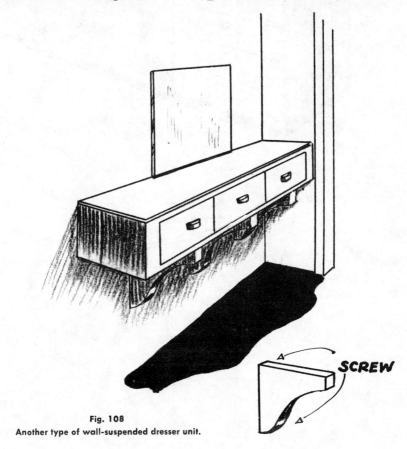

Fig. 108
Another type of wall-suspended dresser unit.

SCREW

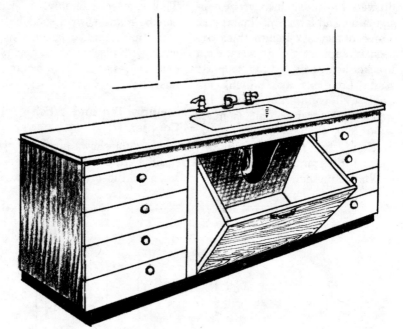

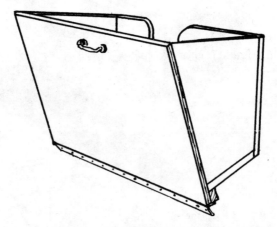

Fig. 109
Drawers and laundry bin enclose wash bowl.

the bin is cut away to clear the basin trap. This may appear to cut down the capacity of the bin, but all you need to do is tack linen loosely over the gap to restore the space you need.

In this unit the apron is flush with the cabinet ends, but there is no stile flanking the drawers. Instead, the drawer fronts also cover the front edges of the sides, as the bottom drawers do the base. Note that the bin is attached by a piano-hinge and swings back into closed position by its own weight. The whole unit is mounted on a 2x4 base set back 3 inches for toe room.

Series 6
ATTIC

Dead Storage

Attic possibilities depend upon clear space dimensions and available floor space under the eaves. In most cases it pays to erect a wall 4 feet high and use the space behind it for dead storage. The rest of the floor space will then have a practical clearance overhead. Fig. 110 shows how this is done. Given sufficient ceiling height, the possibilities for useful built-ins are endless.

Bedroom with Cabineting and Box-Type Beds

Shown in Fig. 111 is a typical attic fitted up as a bedroom for two. The single, box-type beds are on casters so they can be slid under the eaves out of the way when not in use.

When architectural considerations permit (you have to think of the outside of the house as well as the inside), a large window is installed in the gable end. Under it, in the illustration, a desk has been built, flanked by storage cupboards. The tops of the cupboards can be fitted with pads and used as sofas. Otherwise the tops can be hinged on, and chests can be substituted for the cupboards.

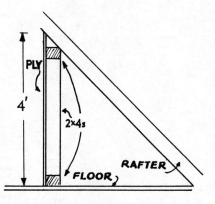

Fig. 110
Four-foot attic wall with dead storage space behind.

If the rafters are open, it is usually a simple matter to nail 6-inch t & g boards directly to them, and to the tie beams to make a ceiling.

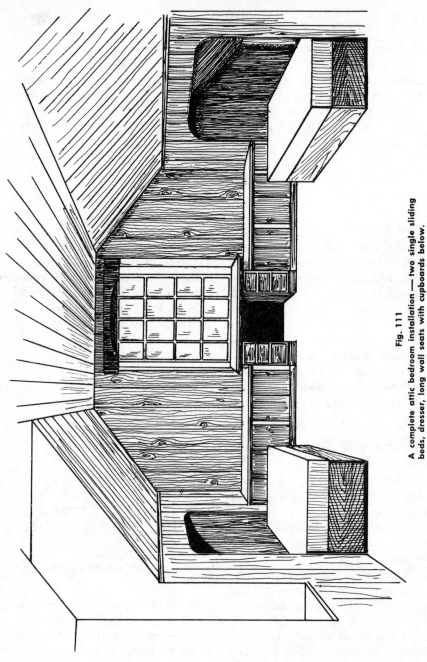

Fig. 111

A complete attic bedroom installation — two single sliding beds, dresser, long wall seats with cupboards below.

Fig. 112
Twin bed arrangement, with shelves and drawers at head, window seat with storage above and below.

Otherwise you can use ½-inch plywood sheets or one of the t & g building boards that come in widths of 10 inches to 18 inches or so. In an old-time attic, with considerable space between rafters, you may have to install heavy furring strips longitudinally and nail the ceiling boards to them at right angles. The wallboard is applied last.

If the tie beams are low, you may be able to raise them, but see a builder about this. When you need extra air space, you can ignore the tie beams (see Fig. 12) and board over the rafters as far as the roof peak. In all cases where the attic is to be occupied, you should insu-

late between the rafters before doing any construction work. If your house has wooden shingles, be sure to leave space for air circulation. In modern houses, you can use batts or roll insulation; in old-

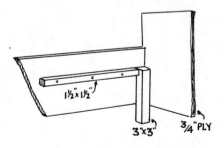

Fig. 113
Supports for mattress slats.

time houses, where the rafter spaces vary, you can install plywood or Celotex over the rafters with reflective insulation between.

Bedroom with Cabinets and Semi-Slideaway Beds

In the illustration (Fig. 112) another attic bedroom is shown, using plywood for the ceiling. Here you have a pair of twin beds that slide their heads three feet under a board forming the top of two sets of drawers and shelves. This top also offers space for reading lamps and books.

A cupboard is built under the eaves by the window. Below the window is a row of small cupboards. The plywood is used in 4x4-foot squares, nailed to alternate rafters or to furring strips. The beds are easy to make from 10- or 12-inch side boards, and plywood head and foot boards. Short legs of 3x3 stiffen the corner joints and terminate in line with the 1½x1½-inch strips that carry the mattress slats, as you see in the detail sketch, Fig. 113. The window seat and cupboard are best built on a 2x3 frame, both for simplicity and strength.

CHAPTER 6

Lumber and Manufactured Sheet-Stock

For the construction of built-in pieces you have the choice of a great variety of materials, and in selecting the right one for any particular job you may save yourself a lot of labor. Some units are better constructed over a stiff frame; others can be built up from boards or sheets that are thick enough to support themselves and withstand ordinary stresses without the need for a frame.

If you use a frame, whether it is made of 1x3s or 2x4s or something heavier, you can, ordinarily, cover it with a light material such as ⅛- or ¼-inch hardboard. The frame, besides giving stiffness to the structure, provides you with something solid to nail into. The common way of combining the advantages of a frame construction with those of lightweight or light section materials is to use heavier boards or panels, ¾-inch or more in thickness. On the other hand, if you are building into a recess where you need no side or back panels, you

can often save material by installing a light frame. Following is a description of materials from which you can choose and so perhaps save time, material, labor and cash.

Lumber

The woods most used for built-ins are: pine, walnut, birch, oak, maple and cedar. Fir is often used for rough, unfinished work and hidden frames. It is not recommended for exposed surfaces, except in the case of some fir plywoods. Normally, pine is preferred.

In estimating how much wood you are going to need for any particular job, you have to consider the actual sizes of the boards you buy. If you get dimension stuff such as 2x3s or 2x4s, you buy by the length — so many lineal feet. In figuring spaces and locations, and in making drawings, remember that these standard dimensions are the sizes of the wood *before it is dressed*. As you buy it, the actual dimensions are:

1x2—$^{25}/_{32}$x1⅝	2x2—1⅝x1⅝
1x3—$^{25}/_{32}$x2⅝	2x3—1⅝x2⅝
1x4—$^{25}/_{32}$x3⅝	2x4—1⅝x3⅝
1x6—$^{25}/_{32}$x5⅝	
1x8—$^{25}/_{32}$x7½	
1x10—$^{25}/_{32}$x9½	

and so on. In the case of tongue-and-groove or shiplap (rabbeted edge) boards, ¼-inch additional is lost for the joint. This means that in a 10-inch t & g board, for example, which has a ¼-inch tongue, the useful width would be only 9⅜ inches.

In buying this kind of wood you do not necessarily have to insist on "clear" knot-free boards, which are expensive. Ordinarily, you can use second grade, and if it is to be painted or papered over, the markings and other defects do not matter too much. It still is best to avoid the so-called knotty pine for any purpose. A rash of black spots over a large surface has little to recommend it.

Plywood and Other Laminated Sheets

In a great many jobs you can save both trouble and cost by using plywood, laminated board or hardboard. These are all available in large sheets, the standard unit being 4 feet x 8 feet, 4x7 feet, 4x12 feet. Thicknesses vary from ⅛-inch to 1 inch.

Plywood consists of three or more sheets of very thin wood bonded together with glue under pressure. The wood is cut by revolving a log against the edge of

a knife. This cuts a thin slice from the circumference so that the grain markings are far different from those of regularly sawn wood — and rarely as interesting. These thin slices are placed one on top of another, with the grains running in alternate directions. This gives the plywood equal strength across and along the sheet. The glue used to bond the sheets may be either water-resistant or actually waterproof. If the built-in structure is to be exposed to excessive dampness or the weather, you should get the waterproof exterior variety.

In the thicker sizes it is not always necessary to have the tremendous strength that many thin plies would give. Therefore, some of the thick boards are made with a lumber core. This type of plywood has the thin plies on the outside; between them is a thick center core composed of strips of solid wood.

Many of these plywoods are available with one or both outer surfaces formed of decorative woods such as mahogany, birch or walnut. Another interesting plywood surface is striated — that is, marked with fine parallel grooves (Fig. 114a). You can get unusual effects by using small panels of this, alternating the direction of the striations. Still another decorative board is a plywood with the soft surface wood burnished away so that the hard grain stands out (Fig. 114b). This is called Etchwood.

Then there is a somewhat dif-

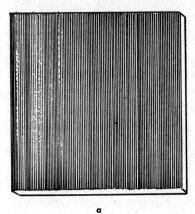

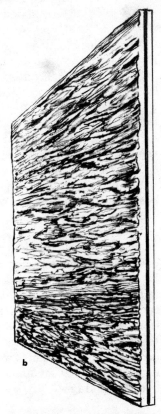

Fig. 114
Striated plywood (a); plywood with soft surface
burnished away to reveal hard grain (b).

Fig. 115
Pieces of Novoply.

ferent type of laminated board, thick and stiff, made of wood flakes. This lightweight, wood-fiber material — its name is Novo-ply — has an interesting surface because of the embedded wood chips (Fig. 115). The surface is light in color and is especially useful as a base for wood or plastic veneer. It makes excellent sliding doors and paneling.

Finally there is a laminated board that is not made of wood veneer or ships. This compressed-fiber board has a light-colored, pebbled surface with inner layers of a delicate blue that identify it as Upson-board. It is available in water-resistant and waterproof types and in thicknesses ranging from $3/8$ inch (6-ply) to 3/16 inch (4-ply). It can be painted or papered. For most cabinet work the material should be applied to a light wood frame.

Hardboards

Another material that is extremely useful in making built-in units of all kinds is known as hardboard. This is a panel material $1/8$ to 5/16 inch thick, made by exploding wood chips into fibers and pressing the fibers, under heat, into dense, rigid boards. No bonding is used except the natural lignin already in the wood. The sheets vary in color from a light brown to almost a chocolate shade, and one is finished dead black. These boards may be smooth on one or both sides or have a pattern em-bossed on one surface. They can be nailed or screwed, drilled (preferably with a twist drill) and sawed.

Probably the most interesting if not the most useful of this series is a dark brown board finished to look like Spanish-grain leather — masonite leatherwood. Most of these hardboards can be bent. Some will stay bent only if fastened to a frame, but others can be bent when damp and will retain the curve when they dry. Others have to be bent under heat. Any of them can be used in a variety of ways. They make especially attractive door panels. You can glue two sheets together to make a heavier board or to form a lip. You can glue sheets to both sides of a board to get a thick section with smooth surfaces such as you would need for a sliding cabinet door. Such a thick section could also be rabbeted to form an exterior panel or a lipped door. In place of a solid core, you can even use a wood frame around the edges and treat it in the same way.

Moldings

Another feature that contributes to the finished look of a built-in is the proper use of moldings. There are stock moldings available in wide variety. You can also buy boards with beaded or chamfered edges (for V-joints) and molded decorative strips or applied decorations such as rosettes and medallions. There is therefore no need for a home-made built-in to look any more amateurish or less attractive than a professionally made one. The trick is in knowing where to use such decoration so you won't get merely a cheap and gaudy effect; the decorations should actually be a part of the complete design and not something that looks as if it had been slapped on as an afterthought.

CHAPTER 7

Finishing and Coloring

Application of Liquid Finishes

BECAUSE you have mahogany furniture in a room does not mean that your built-in piece needs to be faced with that wood. On the contrary, it often happens that the built-in piece should be absorbed into the background by giving it the same color and finish as the general room trim. In other words, instead of being a featured piece of furniture, the built-in can quite properly be considered as part of the walls or the room woodwork and finished in the same way. Mahogany or dark walnut can look well against a light background, but neither mixes very well with pine or any other light grain. So if your built-in must be given a natural (transparent) finish, it should be made fairly dark so it won't clash with the mahogany furniture.

In rooms furnished in mahogany you can, on the other hand, use a plywood with a mahogany facing if you wish. In fact, you can get plywood faced with a large variety of better woods such as birch, maple, walnut or even korina, and color them as you wish.

The finish that you can apply to any built-in piece will depend upon the material from which it is made. For wood surfaces (including plywood) you can use either transparent or opaque finishes. The transparent finishes consist of shellac or varnish, oil-, water- or spirit-stains. The opaques are water and oil paints and enamels. However, there are a number of new finishes available that are well worth trying if you want something both attractive and different.

Any wood that has a hard grain with softer wood between it — such as fir — needs something to prevent the grain ridges showing through an opaque finish. In using stain on such a wood it is necessary also to equalize the absorption to achieve even coloring and a rich finish. A very satisfactory material for this purpose is Firzite. This is available in two types. One solution is clear so that you can use it under stains as a wood sealer. The other is white. It will serve as an undercoat for painted surfaces, in addition to its primary function, and form the base for blond effects that are growing in popularity. White Firzite can be tinted with color.

Not all of the so-called blond finishes need actually be blond. Both the clear and the color finish can be applied in such a manner that the wood grain shows through. A number of paint manufacturers are producing excellent finishes that will give this effect — either by putting on and rubbing off (glazing), or applying in a thinned state. Sapolin Paints, Inc., for example, puts out a series of enamels in color that dry extremely hard and have a hand-rubbed appearance.

If you mix some of this enamel with twice as much turpentine you get the wood-grain effect. This thinned enamel is applied to the smoothly sanded wood. When that coat is dry it is covered with a coat of the "natural" enamel that has no color in it.

Then there is the N-B paint process that lets you make your own wood grain on any surface. All grease has to be removed from the surface by washing with strong Oakite or ammonia solution in warm water. This is washed off and the surface finely sanded. A coat of N-B ground color is applied, and two days later a second

coat is applied which is later sanded. Over this is brushed a thin coat of the N-B graining compound. While it is still wet, most of this is wiped off with cheesecloth. By rubbing in the grain direction with long strokes a grained effect is produced. This is later sealed with a clear finish. This method is actually much less work than it sounds. You must just allow time for the coats to dry.

The staining of woods by modern methods is much simpler than it once was, particularly if you want a satin or glossy finish. One of the easiest methods we have tried is that developed by du Pont. The first step consists of mixing du Pont oil stain with their penetrating wood finish. The proportions are governed by the darkness of the stain required — more stain and less finish give a deeper tone.

This is applied and left to set for five to twenty minutes, depending on the depth of color required. The excess is wiped off, and the rest is left to dry overnight. Then it is sanded with 5/0 garnet paper, and a clear coat of wood finish is applied. The excess of this coat is wiped off after 15 or 20 minutes. Twelve hours later you can burnish the surface with steel wool and finish with paste wax.

An alternative method that lets you regulate your own color calls for adding color to the wood finish instead of using the stain. You can, for instance, use burnt sienna and India red to get a rich mahogany color — or burnt umber and raw sienna for old pine. The wood finish, used alone, gives a satiny clear surface. For a glossy finish, du Pont recommends its Duco clear finish, and its Dulux interior finish for a satiny effect.

For the finishing of hardboards there are available suitable materials in wide variety. You can use lacquer, oil-base paint, latex paint, shellac, penetrating sealers, stain, water-emulsion paint, synthetics, texture paints, and wax.

If you paint or enamel a hardboard, you need a primer or sealer with two paint coats, or an undercoat topped with a coat of enamel. Clear finishes darken the boards somewhat. If you want to keep the original color you will need to use a special sealer, such as Filtex, reduced 50 per cent with benzine or oleum spirits. With two rubbed coats of sealer you then can finish with varnish or lacquer. For a less permanent finish, you can use water-white wax rubbed to a luster.

You can tint or color most hardboards with any non-grain-raising stain; with color-in-oil thinned with turpentine; with dry pigment, or color-in-oil mixed with a clear penetrating sealer; or flat oil paint thinned with turpentine. In each case, the length of time between applying the material and wiping it off will determine the intensity of the color. That fascinating hardboard called Leatherwood (it really looks like leather) can be given a natural finish or else finished in plain colors. A rich effect is secured by giving it a tone-on-tone finish applied in three coats: first, a primer or sealer; second, an interior paint — enamel or lacquer of the desired color; and third, a glazing liquid with added pigment. This last coat is wiped off so that it stays only in the grain depressions of the Leatherwood surface.

Base coats (overall color) and wiping coats that give beautiful and interesting contrasts are these:

BASE COAT	WIPING COAT
Ivory	Yellow ochre
Canary yellow	Dark brown
Emerald green	Dark green
Bright red	Black
Light gray	Black
Light blue	Royal blue
Tan	Dark brown

Similar combinations can be used to bring out the grain effect of Etchwood, though a single wiped-off color is quite effective. Novoply can be stained, but it must be sanded first. Unsanded, it is best finished with either natural or colored wax.

Plastic Veneers

In place of woods with special finishes you can cover almost any wood or metal surface with a plastic veneer. Such veneers are available in a variety of patterns, complete with instructions for their application. You can use veneers that reproduce the grains of rare woods or even the surface patterns of marbles. They are all easy to put on.

INDEX

INDEX

ANCHORS: 24, 47, 83, 97
APRON: 16, 29, 31, 65, 66, 83
ARCHWAY: fillers, 81; trim, 85, 86
ATTACHED FURNITURE: advantages, 18
ATTIC: wall problem, 26; 27, 109, 111, 112

BACKBOARD: 21, 106
BACKSTRIP: 48
BANDING: 19, 73, 75
BASEBOARD: 75, 90
BASEMENT CUPBOARD: 45
BASIC DIMENSIONS: 12, 13, 24
BATHROOM: cabinet, 56; chest, 40; 102, 105
BATTENS: 19, 58, 97
BED: base, 42; bed-desk, 97; box, 109; bunk, 97; construction, 42; head, 101, 102; slideaway, 112; sofa-bunk, 101; twin, 112
BED ORNAMENT: 75
BEDROOM: 109, 112
BENCH SAW: 28
BIN: 47, 59
BOLTS: 12, 24, 40, 41
BOOKCASE: size, 13; 22, 90
BOX: construction, 43, 44, 53; floor storage, 43; lid, 44; seat, 50, 51; wall, 73; 92
BOX TRAY: 42
BRACKETS: 21, 48, 50, 106, 107
BREAD-BOARD: 68
BREAKFAST NOOK: 50
BUILT-INS: advantages, 11, 12; design, 14; detachable, free-standing, 12; planning, 13

CABINET: attaching, 24, 40; ceiling, 60, 61, 64; china, 76, 87; kitchen, 56; partition, 71; poison, 56; stove, 64; wall, 103, 105; workshop, 43; 45, 82, 83, 91, 92, 96, 109, 112
CANOPY: 105
CASCAMITE: 21
CEILING: canopy 105; 23, 24, 25, 60, 91, 109, 111
CELOTEX: 90, 92, 112
CHEST: 109
CHINA CABINET: 76
CLEATS: 19, 25, 50, 66, 68, 83, 97
CLOSET: cleaning, 13; clothes, 13; 85
CONCRETE: nailing to, 47
CONSTRUCTION METHODS: 15, 18
COUNTER TOP: 29, 47, 56, 57, 58, 59, 60, 62, 63, 66, 68, 103, 107

CUPBOARD: basement, 45; corner, 76; secret, 97; 25, 27, 52, 62, 63, 71, 78, 80, 81, 83, 90, 91, 92, 96, 101, 106, 109, 112

DADO: 28, 33, 67, 85, 90
DESIGN: style, 14
DESK: bed-desk, 97; drop, 88; flap, 97; frames, 33; lamp, 64; 35, 64, 66, 87, 89, 96, 101, 109
DINING ROOM: 71, 85
DINING UNIT: apartment type, 74
DOOR: access, 27, 97; box-shaped, 51; cabinet, 35, 37, 39, 42, 58, 60, 63, 64, 116; closet, 36, 39; concertina, 13; flexible, 39; flush, 35; folding, 13; glazed, 33, 60, 61, 78, 80, 83; hinged, 51, 57, 86, 92, 106; sliding, 13, 37, 39, 73, 92, 103; solid, 36, 78; spice-shelf, 56
DOVETAIL JOINT: 32
DOWEL: 18, 47, 61, 97, 105
DRAWERS: dressing unit, 51; dustproof, 42, 88; frame, 32; guides, 32, 33, 42, 57, 64; rollers, 33; side suspension, 32, 33; slides, 32, 33, 42, 57, 60, 61, 64, 67, 97, 105; swinging, 106; 27, 32, 42, 51, 57, 59, 61, 64, 67, 68, 75, 83, 89, 90, 96, 97, 103, 105, 107, 109, 112
DRESSING TABLE: bracket type, 48; legless, 106; 47, 50, 103, 105, 106
DRESSING UNIT: 51

ETCHWOOD: 114, 120

FILTEX: 120
FIRZITE: 118
FLOOR SPACE: 13
FRAMING: door, 62; 18, 20, 25, 27, 43, 56, 63, 75, 87, 88, 96, 105, 112, 113, 116
FURRING: 25, 111, 112
FINISHES: 118, 119, 120 (see also Paint)

GALLERY: 51, 75
GAME ROOM: 101
GIRT: 25
GLAZING BARS: 78
GLUE BLOCKS: 31, 76
GYPSUM BOARD: (see Plasterboard)

HAMPER: linen, 103
HANGERS: 41
HARDBOARD: 45, 52, 63, 83, 85, 87, 88, 105, 113, 116
HI-FI: 96
HINGES: butt, 58; installing, 58; piano, 106, 109; tee, 44; 58, 76

IRONING BOARD: 71

JOINTS: 15, 18, 19, 20, 96
JOINT FASTENINGS: 20

KITCHEN: 59, 71
KNEE-ROOM: 50

LADDER: 97
LAUNDRY BIN: 52, 107, 109
LEGS: 21, 44
LID: 44
LINOLEUM: 58, 61
LIVING ROOM: 81, 82, 87, 92
LUMBER: dimensions, 56, 76, 81, 83
87, 91, 113, 114

MASONITE: Leatherwood, 116, 120
MASONRY: 21
MEDICINE CABINET: 53
MIRROR: frame, 52; vanity, 105; 50,
53, 103, 105, 106
MITER: box, 33; 23
MOLDING: cornice or "sprung," 23;
19, 28, 35, 61, 75, 76, 78, 80, 81, 83,
86, 90, 106, 116
MUNTIN: 61

NAILS: upholstery, 51; 20, 21, 22, 28,
56
NAILING BASE: 43, 45, 47, 56, 60, 66,
76, 87, 88, 90, 96, 103, 109
NAILING STRIP: 24, 61
NOVOPLY: 88, 116

PAINT: asphalt, 47; 50, 71, 73, 75, 85,
96, 114, 119, 120
PANEL: decorative, 85; floor, 87; radio,
92; roof, 87; 35, 73, 88, 97, 104, 116
PARTITION: 71, 87
PEDESTAL: 80
PHONOGRAPH: 88, 90
PILASTER: 80
PILLOW SUPPORT: 97
PLASTERBOARD: 82, 86
PLASTIC: 58, 61, 63, 71, 73, 75, 85, 107,
116, 120
PLASTIC WOOD: 20, 28
PLAYROOM: 92
PLINTH: 75, 76
PLUGS: wall, 21
PLYWOOD: edge treatment, 19; stri-
ated, 71, 115; 36, 43, 44, 47, 51, 52, 56,
57, 58, 63, 66, 73, 75, 82, 83, 85, 90,
92, 96, 102, 106, 111, 112, 114, 118
POWER TOOLS: use of, 15
PRESSED BOARD: (see Hardboard)
PROJECTOR-SCREEN: 92

RABBET: 32, 33, 35, 88
RACKS: 59, 63, 67

RADIO: 88, 90
RAFTERS: 27, 109, 111, 112
ROOF INSULATION: 27, 111, 112
ROOM DIVIDER: 26, 96
ROOM PLANNING: 12

SCREWS: use of, 21; 28, 31
SHEETROCK: (see Plasterboard)
SHELVES: adjustable, 28; book, 97;
cupboard, 83, 85; kitchen, clothes
closet, 13; pullout, 68; sliding, 64;
spice, 56; support(s), 28, 76; 21, 25, 27,
28, 29, 42, 45, 47, 50, 52, 53, 59, 63,
67, 71, 76, 85, 86, 89, 92, 101, 102, 112
SIDEBOARD: 73, 81
SINK: board, 63; 63
SOFA: 109
SOFA-BUNK: 101
SPACKLE: 19
SPEAKER: 96
SPICE SHELF: 56
STORAGE: box, 43; cupboard, 76;
dead, 109; ironing board, 71; rack, 67,
90; record, 88; reorganizing, 13; 11,
12, 27, 42, 59, 60, 64, 81, 85, 87, 92,
97, 101, 105
STRUCTURAL DETAILS: 21
STUDS: framing, 25; location, 24
STYLE: 14
SWEDISH PUTTY: 19

TABLE TOP: drop, 71; 29, 44
TIE-BEAMS: 27, 109, 111
TELEVISION: 92
TOENAILING: 25, 48, 57, 60
TOGGLE BOLTS: 24, 41
TOWEL RAIL: 63
TRAFFIC LANES: 12
TRAYS: 51, 63, 64
TRIM: door, 85; metal, 60; 18, 22, 53,
83, 86

UPHOLSTERY: 51
UPSON BOARD: 116
VALANCE: 105
VARNISH: 19
VENEERS: 120

WALLBOARD: 25, 26, 27, 51, 52, 83,
86, 91, 111
WALL NICHE: 52
WALL PLATE: 25, 27
WALL PLUG: 40, 41
WALLS: bad, 25; 18, 26
WARDROBE: 87
WASHBASIN: 107
WELDWOOD: 21
WINDOW-WALL: 90
WINDOW SEAT: 91
WOOD PUTTY: 20
WOODS: 113